D·E·C·I·D·I·N·G

Self-deception in life choices

TOD STRATTON SLOAN

Methuen · New York and London

Published in 1987 in the USA by
Methuen & Co.
in association with Methuen, Inc.
29 West 35th Street, New York
NY 10001

First published in 1987 by
Methuen & Co. Ltd
11 New Fetter Lane, London
EC4P 4EE

Typeset by Rowland
Phototypesetting Ltd
Bury St Edmunds, Suffolk

Printed in the
United States of America

*British Library Cataloguing in
Publication Data*

Sloan, Tod Stratton
Deciding: self-deception in life
choices.
1. Decision-making
I. Title
153.8'3   BF441

ISBN 0-416-91560-4

*Library of Congress Cataloging in
Publication Data*

Sloan, Tod Stratton, 1952–
Deciding: self-deception in life
choices.
Bibliography: p.
Includes index.
1. Decision-making.
2. Decision-making – Case studies.
3. Interviews.
I. Title.
BF441.S6   1986   153.8'3
86-8623
ISBN 0-416-91560-4

TO MARÍA CARLOTA

TABLE OF CONTENTS

ACKNOWLEDGMENTS

I argue in these pages that decisions are not private and personal accomplishments. Neither is this book. Every idea presented is the synthesis of conversations, dialogues, readings, and life experience. To acknowledge this creative "intersubjectivity," I wish to thank my friends and colleagues in Ann Arbor for their critical support for this research, especially: George Rosenwald, Randy Earnest, Barnaby Barratt, Gary Gregg, Michael Jackson, Donald Brown, Jack Meiland. To those who read early versions of the manuscript and from whose advice and/or encouragement I benefited, a hearty thanks: John Broughton, Larry Wrightsman, Rae Carlson, Kenneth Gergen. My gratitude also to the courageous volunteer participants in my research, for helping me figure out what I needed to investigate. For clerical assistance beyond the call of duty: Lucy Mylar, Karen DeShong, and Vickie Booth. A portion of my research expenses were covered by the Department of Psychology at the University of Michigan and by a Faculty Research Grant from the University of Tulsa Graduate School. And, finally, a special thanks to the cherished friends who have sustained me through the years.

The woman asked, "Are you happy, Father?"
The father shook his head. Then, as though the
gesture were not sufficient answer, he said, "No."
"Have you some idea about how one might live?"
The father: "Oh, cut it out. Don't say such
things."

Peter Handke, *The Left-Handed Woman*

FOREWORD

George C. Rosenwald

Our common history descends from a disastrous decision: Adam and Eve chose badly and paid for it. We are living with the consequences, determined each of us to choose more wisely, to make decisions that will retrieve the lapsed bliss. Our own choices seem harder to us of course than that first one. But we receive no leniency. Make the wrong move, we are told, and your life will be spoiled.

How early the agony begins! The mere child is expected to choose among alternatives placed before it as though by divine authority. And as it chooses correctly, it finds favor in the parental countenance. It learns not merely to choose correctly but that correct choice is the key to happiness.

The joint force of mythic and familial morality persuades us that choosing wisely is our unavoidable duty, our gateway to fulfillment. Not to be free to choose would mean not to be human. Accordingly people who squirm in the throes of indecision are pitied as weaklings. Freud gave us the pathography of *Zweifelsucht*, doubting mania.

In reading Dr. Sloan's book, we begin to suspect that wisdom gravitates to doubt. Not being able to choose is the philosophical mind's subjective signal that it has finally grasped the complexity and obscurity of its situation. We recall that it took a warrior to undo the Gordian Knot. Decisiveness is the self-directed callousness with which we smother subtlety, a microsuicide perhaps. Yet resoluteness is considered a virtue. So powerful is the moral pressure to make smart moves that a wise psychiatrist had to urge a young doctor not to decide merely to have made a decision.

We suppose that we think out the solution to a dilemma. But what we call thinking is both more and less than it seems – less because of its imperfect rationality, more because the vindication we often hope to squeeze from a right decision cannot be won with mere thoughts. This book opens our eyes to the multiple agendas that wait upon the decision. People often expect to satisfy not only themselves, but an implicit audience. They attempt to bring order not only into the world they inhabit, but also their psychic households. They often want to settle not only the issue at hand, but all issues forever, not only to create a better life, but to achieve immortality. No decision can live up to such expectations – especially since, as the author shows, who one is limits what one can decide. This is why decisions are so draining, why they seem so overblown in retrospect. *Post decisionem omne animal triste.*

From Dr. Sloan's excerpted life stories we learn that so-called major life decisions draw their significance not merely from unconscious conflicts, but from the anxiety of ignorance. At the moment of deciding we simulate omniscience. If we really knew the consequences of our available choices, we could declare our preference. In truth, however, a life decision is called major precisely when we do not know, when we are about to overreach ourselves, plunging into uncertainty. The technological mentality offers us flow charts, algorithms of choice behavior, and decision trees as though these could enrich our wretched data base. The case histories in this volume serve as fitting rejoinders to the simplicities of decision theory. They sober us up, give the reader an illumination, a guidance without the usual cheerful prescriptions of how-to books.

The ignorance we face is neither the theologian's imploring us to humility nor the poet's contemplating the heavens. It reigns in the gap between what society demands of individuals and what it allows them: To thine own self be true! But with what? The men and women in this book feel under command to lead a worthy life, one that is truly theirs and no one else's, and yet they don't know where to look. The consequences of various options are inscrutable, out of control. Lo! the poor Indian had it easier. He knew all he needed to know to please his gods and himself, and what he didn't know would not diminish the dignity of his minimalist choices. If the quarry escaped, if the crops failed, if he succumbed in combat – these were not tallied as the outcomes of poor decisions. We see now that the ignorance we face is ignorance made. The decision tree is not the tree of life.

The readers of this book must not expect instruction in deciding. If anything, they will find the author sympathetic with their plight. When approaching difficult choices, we are handicapped by our misconceptions of what a decision involves. Traditional psychological approaches to decision theory, far from enlightening us about this matter, tend to abet our rationalistic illusions. This book goes a long way toward helping people, one day, to face complexity without perplexity.

INTRODUCTION: THE PROBLEM OF CHOICE

For several years now, I have been fascinated by that mysterious process whereby we are able to rise above confusion, and put an end to seemingly endless deliberation to announce, "I have made a decision!" When we are uncertain about the future and when we hardly know what we want in the present, the fact of coming to a decision would seem to be quite an achievement. At crucial turning-points of life – at junctures where we know that there will be no easy turning back – the accomplishment of deciding is even more impressive.

Yet the decisions we make come to be blamed, often unjustly, for subsequent suffering and dissatisfaction. What looked like a wonder-fully rational decision may soon be viewed as the worst moment of self-deception in one's life. The spontaneous and self-assured foray into a new realm of endeavor might prove to be the first step on the road to self-destruction.

The possibility of developing a psychology of major life decisions is complicated by the fact that any significant choice has an *ethical* dimension. The deciding individual is obviously embedded in social, cultural, interpersonal, and historical contexts, all of which are affected, however slightly, by the final choice. Simultaneously, the train of thought engaged in by a person trying to make up his or her mind is dominated by the constraints and opportunities, values and norms, that characterize those interwoven contexts. The complexity of deciding is overwhelming. Our task will be to find some structure within that complexity.

One hardly needs to be enamored of existential psychology and other philosophical questions about life to be concerned with the problem of authenticity in major life decisions. The problem of being true to oneself plagues most of us at crucial turning-points. We ask, how is it possible to reconcile these conflicting parts of myself? How do I know I'm not fooling myself? What is the right thing for *me* to do? These are the questions that led to the research on which this book is based.

To find answers, I was compelled to examine directly the nature of major life decisions. There was no way to do this in the laboratory. I went directly to people who could tell me about important decisions they had made or were in the process of making. I spent seventy hours interviewing fifteen volunteer adult subjects and five years rummaging around in the transcripts of those interviews. The object of my research soon shaped up as a multifaceted *experience* that had to be approached from many angles.

In the typical case, stripped of its many variations, a "major life decision" is set up by a dilemma that emerges in the midst of a relatively stable pattern of involvements. The dilemma is disturbing or, at least, challenging, in that its resolution could require a trans-formation of commitments, plans, self-concepts, and central activities. Sooner or later, we come to see ourselves as having to make up our minds. Usually, but not always, we have heard how others faced with such a decision chose to resolve it. It is also often clear from the outset which particular outcome would be preferable to others and to ourselves. Still, we are unable to *decide*.

A certain amount of what we call "thinking" is devoted to the issue at hand. Pros and cons of alternatives are examined, usually unsys-tematically. Fantasies of the consequences of alternatives are unraveled in the imagination. New possibilities are conceived and rejected as impractical or perhaps kept for further consideration. The reactions of others are considered. Frequently, persons directly implicated by the decision are not included in the deliberations. Clues as to the best course of action are taken from a wide range of sources, including casual conversations, trivial events, horoscopes, natural omens.

This deliberation continues intermittently, often despite the fact that we might later say, "I knew how I was going to decide all along." Then, with no great increment in certainty, it becomes possible or necessary to decide, to make a commitment to a particular course of action.

Afterward, there may be doubts or regrets about the direction taken. In many cases, we come to think that we actually had no choice, that we did the only thing we could. In others, we are certain that another route, "the road not taken," would have been highly preferable.

Such is the terrain to be clarified in this book.

Before plunging into the nitty-gritty of decision making, we will do well to stand back to obtain at least a partial bird's-eye view of the context which helped to make decisions an issue for psychologists. A useful dimension of life to begin with is our sense of options and constraints. The social and technological revolutions of the twentieth century seem to have vastly increased the options open to the individual. Lifestyles previously impractical, or reserved for elites, are now open to millions. The combinations and permutations of possibilities make individuality a reality many struggle to cope with now, instead of a lofty ideal to be attained. A cultural emphasis on the construction of a meaningful individual lifestyle induces a hyperconsciousness about choices. The existence of options exerts a pressure to make decisions, a pressure which few of us seem to handle in a completely satisfying manner.

In times when social structures and cherished values had longer lifespans, individuals could ground their engagement in the world on apparently solid foundations. Given that support, I imagine, they could devote attention to the practical matters and dilemmas of everyday life: how to fix the plow, where to find more food, how to get back at the neighbors, or what to do with the ailing grandfather. It is impossible to enumerate the factors which have changed this scene, but the crumbling of religion in the face of science, immigration, the incredible augmentation of communication systems from books to satellite news, the reduction of time spent at work, the spread of literacy and the rise of public education figure prominently. Whatever the causes, there is now a population of individuals who have actually *seen* hundreds of ways of living and who must, in turn, make choices for themselves, and generally without much feeling of groundedness in their values.

In one sense it was harder to know that one *had* to choose between being a farmer, a priest, or a merchant, but in another it can be immensely difficult to select a career when the occupational catalog lists thousands of niches into which one could stuff a life of work. Similarly, it must have been difficult to have one's marriage arranged, or to *have* to get married shotgun style, but the current scene makes choosing partners for intimacy into a confusing maze which, while contributing to broader interpersonal experiences, certainly does not spare the individual from emotional pain or loss.

In particular, the individuals commonly referred to as "young adults" have a difficult time with the important life decisions they are expected to make as they move out of the preparation-for-life phase into early adulthood. Consider, for example, this list of "keys to your future fulfillment and happiness" one should make "thoughtful decisions" about, according to Crystal and Bolles' *Where Do I Go From Here With My Life?* (1974):

> where you want to live
> kinds of people you want to work with
> activities you will enjoy
> working and living conditions you really like
> ideal job specifications
> values you hold important and beyond compromise
> your major interests
> issues you want to solve, ends to attain
> care of your family and what that requires
> your future lifestyle, and your loved ones' involvement in it
> financial needs and desires
> educational desires
> alternatives and options to safeguard

The authors tell us that once one knows oneself and the realities of the world of work (the major concern of the book), one is "then ready to decide exactly what you most want to accomplish in that world. This requires a series of carefully sequenced decisions . . . on the various matters which will be of greatest significance to you for your future" (p. 72). I have become fairly pessimistic about such claims.

Even experienced adults have a hard time with such decisions and for all their sincerity and resolve, young adults, with rare exceptions, are mainly groping, grasping, stabbing, clinging, or longing. All talk of abundant options and possibilities needs to be critically re-evaluated in their case. Possibilities only have meaning in terms of experiences. Young adults have been systematically prevented from having many of the experiences which could render their initial decisions less opaque. For example, schoolwork is not particularly conducive to knowing what real jobs are like. Nor do the models provided by one's parents and siblings constitute an especially good preparation for adult intimacy. And as far as the other matters are concerned (such as where to live, job specifications, uncompromisable values), the picture is more grim.

Young adults are not alone in having important decisions to make, although the urgency and difficulty of decision making weigh on them most. Adults in the middle and later years, certainly feel compelled to make hard decisions at times and typically wish they could reverse earlier decisions. So despite appearances, the constraints on adult decision making are as intense as they have always been. Limitations due to character, social class, gender, ethnicity, location, the body, scarcity, finances, and the like black out the glowing accounts we often hear regarding life chances in a free society.

It is simplistic to think of freedom merely in terms of opportunities and constraints. It is much more than that. When we look at freedom as having something to do with being true to some essential aspects of ourselves or with becoming "who we are," or as pertaining to "authenticity," the problem of deciding deepens. Even in a world of plentiful opportunities and minimized constraints, effective engagement is elusive. It is difficult to know what will work, and what is worth working toward. Deciding becomes a strategizing, a compromising, a means of situating oneself in and against a complex of social relations . . . hence, much more than a way of selecting among attractive alternatives.

In response to this complex and contradictory world, an ethic has developed which justifies a sort of "rolling over" in the face of social buffetings. This ethic says that life is about changing. The authentic individual accepts change as a part of life. Given sufficient courage, any change induces growth and can become a "learning experience." We find this ethic expressed most frequently by authors influenced by the humanistic-existential movement in psychology. To quote one of the better popular treatments of the problem:

Change is the way we build our own future.

Change is not, however, the transformation of oneself into something entirely different, but rather its expansion into a more vivid realization of what we already are.

Change, both within ourselves and in the world we inhabit, is inevitable and unending. We can choose to see the possibilities it offers as a reflection of our values – or simply give ourselves over to it passively . . . .

The urge toward change is invariably accompanied by the fear of changing. To stand still requires the courage to defend what you now are; to risk change requires the still greater courage of discovering what you might become.

The price of change is real – and as unique – as the necessity for change. Yet that tuition is finally the only investment worth making

– so long as you know what it is, and are willing to pay it as the price of growth.

(Grossman, 1978, pp. 91–2)

One obvious question: Does changing one's life always imply growth?

Another approach links decisions to changing *and* goal-setting. An advertisement for a recent self-help book reads:

Learn to change for the better. Fulfillment is nothing more than the setting up and attaining of goals. It is important whether your goals are material or spiritual, social or sexual, long-term or short-term, simple or complex.

Is there really a strategy for goal-attainment which would work for nearly any goal? Are life changes and associated decisions primarily instrumental actions, techniques for achieving practical ends? Merely ways of shaping or molding oneself?

We clearly have nothing to lose and much to gain by asking: What does it mean to *decide*? How are decisions related to character development? Why is self-misunderstanding so prevalent?

Notes on method

This examination of major life decisions is intended to contribute to the development of a critical and interpretive psychology. The term critical is drawn from the usage associated with the Institute for Social Research at Frankfurt, Germany from 1930 to 1950 (see Jay, 1973; Held, 1980, for historical background). Its members included Herbert Marcuse, Theodor Adorno, Max Horkheimer and more recently, Jürgen Habermas. The "critical theory" developed by these social philosophers insists that knowledge cannot be evaluated apart from the social interests it serves, that theory and practice are intimately linked, and that the free development of individuals is contingent on the rational organization of the society in which they participate. Their works are characterized by an interest in the critique of ideology, a practice which led them to investigate an extremely wide range of topics from obscure philosophies and literatures to popular trends in television, radio, architecture, and astrology.

Habermas (1968) distinguishes three interests that science can be said to serve. The first is an interest in technical control and instrumental action, pursued by the "empirical-analytic" sciences. Characterized by a positivistic methodological stance, these sciences are largely inappropriate to the understanding of human interaction and social reality. When these interests inform research in the human sciences, the view of human life which follows could generally be characterized as reductionistic, control-oriented, and reifying (that is, denying human capacities for self-reflection, for example, making individuals into mere objects for manipulation, or assuming that qualities of individuals in current conditions are essential to human nature). Academic psychology in the West grounds itself primarily in this sort of paradigm.

A second approach embodied in the historical-hermeneutic sciences attempts to comprehend life practices through interpretive hypotheses which can be debated and changed in the light of conceptions that more adequately grasp the complexity and uniqueness of experience. This approach emphasizes "intersubjectivity," the dialogic relation between individuals in which intentions are communicated. The primary goal of the hermeneutic sciences is the understanding of others not as objects, but as subjects who can express themselves meaningfully, however limited this capacity. Methods appropriate to this goal involve interpretation and understanding, rather than explanation in cause-effect terms (Bleicher, 1980).

Finally, Habermas identifies an interest which is frequently ignored in pursuing the other two interests. This is referred to as an emancipatory interest. Here, the aim is to free subjects from forces which limit their capacity for reflection and to uncover and destroy conditions in which domination, oppression, and ideology constrain autonomy. The key to this process is self-understanding attained through critical self-reflection, likened to reflection in the psychoanalytic dialogue. In consequence of this process, conceptions of the world and action within it are modified in a direction more likely to result in human fulfillment.

The issues surrounding this characterization of scientific interests are complex (Held, 1980). They have been introduced at this point because it is important to establish an understanding regarding the interests which inform this project. We are attempting to describe and understand specific experiences of major life decisions through the application and development of interpretive categories or concepts. This differs from the aim of the empirical-analytic model of science which could, for example, be justifiably concerned with demonstrating the aggregate preconditions of certain career choices or exploring the impact of the national economy on decisions to relocate, and so forth.

An interpretive approach must resist the tendency to move toward abstract general explanations – especially if such factors like the trends of the national economy or class position are not understood as they operate in the lives of particular individuals. This is not to say that an abstracting move should never be made. Mediating concepts are essential to communication. Some argue that to understand human experience accurately, one must remain at the level of a faithful "phenomenological" description. They would encourage, for example, using as much of an interviewee's personal language as possible and incorporating only concepts the subject himself would employ. This aim assumes that subjects are capable of accurately representing their experience in language and that our understanding of others develops across a vacuum, unmediated by concepts. Both assumptions are clearly untenable (Spence, 1982). These conditions render descriptive analyses insufficient.

We need to know how people misunderstand their situations and their decisions, and why they do. The latter goal would seem to call for an analysis of factors which are not immediately apparent to the subject, nor obvious to an observer. It is in uncovering the obstacles to self-understanding that forces which subvert personal choices are likely to be discovered.

A grasp of influences of this order is the first step toward the fulfillment of the emancipatory interest of a critical psychology. In examining specific experiences of major life decisions, we will develop a sense of the psychological constraints on the rationality of the deciding subject as well as the social, material, and practical influences.

QUESTIONS ABOUT DECIDING: THE CONTEXT OF CHARACTER

Even a casual stroll through a museum of modern art is sufficient to convince one that twentieth-century representations of the human form reflect the contradictions, distortions, blockages, and absences of everyday experience. What artists manage to express, the rest of us live out in a largely unconscious fashion. In their works, artists creatively objectify hesitation, self-reassurance, anxiety, regret — the entire landscape of the inner world. It is on this uncertain terrain, this quicksand of confusion, that questions about deciding arise.

It is not at all difficult to raise questions about decisions. Decisions are prompted by questions. How may we know which questions about deciding will take us along enlightening paths? To avoid the catastrophe of wasting time on pointless questions, a preliminary attempt to frame the object of our inquiry would seem wise. Using the following passage from a series of life history interviews with a woman in her late twenties, we can make our first approach to the slippery phenomena of decision making:

> I came up with a big decision. I don't know if I told you this before, but when my ex-husband and I split up, I came to the conclusion that I would never date a married man. Our marriage had broken up because of his affair with Suzie, so I wasn't about to do that to somebody else. But now I've been seeing a married man for almost a

year [laughs]. That was a very big turn-around in my life. I deliberated about that for a long time. I met this man at the plant. We started talking to each other at work and going out to lunch together. It started as a friendship and things just kind of grew from that. It's been very beneficial to me, but if things don't work out in this relationship with Carl, I don't think I'll ever put myself through it again. It was a big decision. It took me a long time.

What do we have here? For this subject — let's call her Sherry — a "big decision" implies a clash of personal values, a major change of attitude, a form of self-contradiction. She puts the word "decision" on the moment in which she adopts a new stance toward her self and her world.

What is hiding beneath this word that fits so neatly on that complex moment? I asked her, "What went through your mind as you tried to make that decision?":

I remembered a lot of things that happened to me when my ex started going out on me, when our whole marriage started breaking apart. As I thought about these things, I stopped my whole program, both physically and mentally. I just closed down and avoided people just to think about it. I had to come to some kind of conclusion that would be fair – to what I thought was right and what Carl's wife would feel was right and what Carl would feel was right. It was a big turmoil for a really long time.

Most of us associate the word decision with this sort of intense thinking. The thinking is absorbing and time-consuming. We stop in our tracks. Our routine is interrupted, however briefly. We seek a *conclusion* that will allow us to move forward with a compromise in mind. Sherry would not let herself merely *act*. She paused in order to act with justification for a problematic action.

What is most puzzling about this retrospective account is that for all Sherry's emphasis on the rational process that led her to a thoughtful conclusion, one senses an unspoken *urge* to arrive at exactly that conclusion.

It could be, of course, that Sherry is mainly seeking to justify an action that she knows is not likely to be socially accepted. She builds a case for herself, a defense. She affirms that she *did* think before acting. She claims to have come to a logical conclusion. At the time of the interview, I must not have been satisfied with this preliminary account of the decision for I asked her to reconstruct as carefully as possible her thoughts about the issues involved in her decision. Her response:

It all started as a thinking process. When I started seeing Carl at the plant, he told me he was married right off the bat. I figured it was all right since we were in the plant and there were so many people around us. We started going to lunch together and just talking. He told me about his wife and we started rapping about our lifestyles and other stuff. About six weeks after we met each other, Carl asked me to go out. I just looked at him and said, "Hey, it's one thing seeing you here at the plant, but it's another thing if I were to go out with you." He asked why and I said, "Because you're married." And he says, "Why should it make any difference if I see you in here or out there? I just want to get you in a setting where we can sit down and talk in private." I said, "I'm going to have to think about this one." He knew why. I had told him the reason why I got divorced and I told him about my vow not to date a married man. So I started thinking about it realistically.

In this passage, Sherry helps us to stumble toward an extraordinarily important realization about decision making. Far from being the "internal," "psychological," "thinking" process we imagine it to be, we will continually discover that the experiential foundations of a particular decision lie in complex networks of social relations. We may refer to this social dimension of deciding as its *intersubjectivity*. The rhetoric of decision making – "*I* made up my mind," "*I* came up with a big decision," "*I've* finally decided . . ." – obscures this struggle between human subjects and pretends that *I* am in control, that I *will* such and such to be the case, and that *my* rationality brings me to want this.

Sherry went on to portray her "realistic thinking" about her dilemma as follows:

Just because a married person goes out on his partner, it doesn't mean that the woman he's going to is at fault. There's a lot of things that must go on in a marriage to cause one of the partners to go out of that boundary to seek companionship from another person, so step by step, I broke my marriage up again in my mind, to find out I was very, very bitter, not that Tom went out on me. I hated Suzie [his lover]! It wasn't that I hated Suzie, because I really didn't know her. I really hated Tom [laughs] but Suzie was the excuse. Suzie was the only person I could blame at the point that we broke up. So I really had to do a lot of soul searching. I even tried going to church and praying about it. It didn't work [laughs]. So it took me about a month to tell Carl I would go out and he said "Fine. Saturday night?" I said, "Boy, that's quick."

Here we come face to face with the ultimate paradox of decision making: the conscious "rational" process which we call "deciding" is apparently *not* the final voice in some choices. Sherry's deliberation led her to consider her bitterness about her ex-husband's unfaithfulness and her anger at the other woman. She also attempts to relieve herself of guilt by concluding that she is not the cause of Carl's potential unfaithfulness – the problem lies in his marriage. She thus offers one "pro" and one "con." Her visit to the church was most likely a final effort to fend off a conclusion toward which she felt compelled, not by the force of her reasoning (since it pointed primarily against involvement with Carl), but by a pressure she is unable to understand, a logic which disrupts her attempt to be reasonable.

The paradoxical phenomenon illustrated by Sherry's retrospective account is known in philosophical literature as *self-deception*. It is characterized by an inability to avow one's primary motives and is thus known colloquially as "lying to oneself" or even "fooling oneself." This disavowal is an unconscious process which permits one to deny responsibility for an act and its consequences. Rationalization fills in the gap between action and responsibility: "It's not *my* fault he's going out on his wife."

Any discussion of self-deception leads implicitly to ethical questions. Any psychology of decision making which pretends to be free of such implications is fooling itself. Our strategy will be to avoid judgment of the helpful volunteers who participated in this study by asking not, "Is Sherry's decision right or wrong?" but "How does she come to make this particular decision?" We will be able, given the latter attitude, to understand what makes self-deception possible in each of us and what may be done about it. We must be careful in this process to focus neither on the morality of the decisions examined here, nor on the healthiness or craziness involved. Those dimensions of judgment are best suspended for reasons which become apparent shortly.

It would be a cheap trick to attribute Sherry's decision to self-deception and leave it at that. Our responsibility is to push until this decision is more or less *understood*. Decisions, especially important ones, are not arbitrary – they have *meanings*. This means simply that decisions strive to fulfill intentions, desires, wishes. We basically need to know, first, how people manage to have wishes of which they are unaware and, then, how these influence decisions such that "self-deception" is a common experience.

I have said that to understand a decision, one must grasp its meaning. This is not a matter of tracing patterns of cause and effect, or of describing it from a subjective point of view. The meaning of a decision goes beyond its immediate referents. It is not only "about" the specific changes that it brings about in a person's life.

Decisions derive meaning from the contexts which *determine* them, from the systems of relations a subject works within and against. The intentions to be fulfilled by a decision could only make sense in terms of such contexts. As obvious as this may sound, standard approaches to the psychology of decision making often ignore one context or another, the consideration of which would seem essential to articulating the basis either for an understanding of the dilemma at hand or coming to a sensible choice.

A useful analogy can be drawn between decisions and words. A word derives its meaning from its place in a sentence, a grammar, a work, a dialect, a communication, or a language. The word's meaning is determined by these and other contexts. The word bears a relation to the reality it signifies, but that relationship is mediated by its embeddedness in contexts. We cannot assume that the determining forces are the same in the case of decisions; but the analogy holds with regard to the multiplicity of relevant contexts. It is clear that a decision may be misconstrued as aiming to accomplish only a narrow practical intention, but to accept this, as many individuals and several theories of decision making do, would fortify self-deceptive tendencies.

The contexts of deciding, then, inasmuch as they constitute meanings, are susceptible to specific modes of reflective understanding. Put simply, the meanings of a decision can be thought about. A decision is no mystery, but until its contexts and the relations between them are specified, it is likely to remain perplexing. There must be ways of thinking about decisions which will dissolve at least certain regions of that perplexity.

The main context to which we will turn in the search for the meaning of Sherry's decision is delineated by the terms "character" or "personality." (I prefer the former for its connotation of rigidity and its ethical dimension; the latter is used so globally and carelessly as to be worthless.)

To understand Sherry's or anyone's character, it is essential to take a brief detour into psychoanalysis − the field pioneered by Freud. The literature of Freudian theory is vast, intricate, and controversial, even with regard to its basic elements. But if we ask "how people manage to have motives of which they are unaware," it is imperative to consider the perspective offered by the cumulative experience of those who make the exploration of the unconscious mind their business.

Freudian theory consists of conceptual construction designed to account for observations and experiences afforded by the analytic situation – the peculiar dialogue between a freely associating patient and an analyst who listens and interprets. The accumulated wisdom of psychoanalytic practice indicates that actions have meanings which are not at first acknowledged by the subject. A reason offered to account for an action may turn out to be only one of many actual motives and, in some instances, can even contradict a primary conscious wish fulfilled through that action. A generous gesture may mask hostility if, for example, the gift is burdensome to its recipient. In decision making, the possibility that actions are founded on motives which are not acknowledged (whether repressed or merely preconscious) poses a very serious problem. These unconscious motives are grounded in character, the pattern for which is established in early life experiences.

In a nutshell, this is how the formation of character may be understood: in infancy, a child is unable to distinguish itself from the world around it, nor from its caretakers. The child begins to experience its separateness in the alternating presence and absence of parents, food, toys, or as it gets hurt and feels pain from some external or internal source. The psyche develops partly in a defensive reaction to these early separation experiences. The abilities to fantasize absent objects or persons, to remember and to recognize all serve to ease the discomfort of this phase.

The child learns that it has little or no control over others in its environment and becomes aware of its dependency. It tries to avoid jeopardizing its existence through actions which might provoke punishment and pain. Certain desires, varying from stage to stage in the child's development, have to be banned entirely from conscious consideration because their expression too frequently brings on pain, punishment, or disapproval. Such forbidden desires are associated with the physiologically determined feeling-states of anxiety or fear.

Subsequently, the child automatically moves away from images or representations of prohibited actions or objects. These "repressed wishes" remain unchanged by later experience and "insist" toward expression so continuously that important features of character are established to defend against their interference and to find substitute gratifications. A collection of co-ordinated "defense mechanisms" thus forms the core of what we call character.

We can describe the process of character formation in a slightly different manner by focusing on the process called "socialization." As a child is prepared for participation in civilized life, it is left with images of itself and others which are either positively or negatively toned. These images, or "self-and-other representations," arise directly from paradigmatic interactions between the child and its "significant others" (Kernberg, 1977). A set of positively toned self-and-other images form the basis of conscious identifications: I am strong like my father, giving like my mother, etc. Unconscious images of the self as "bad" (for harboring unacceptable aggressive or sexual impulses toward others) also guide action. The anxiety aroused as these images and associated impulses seek expression generates a system of "ego defenses" (A. Freud, 1937) or "character armor" (Reich, 1945). However we designate these structures, they serve to shift attention away from aims that are tabooed in a characteristic manner. The various moves which are most common are catalogued in any primer of Freudian psychology.

Defensive operations are largely automatic. There may be a vague sense of trying to "slip something by" or "tricking" somebody else in some cases, but the defenses which influence decision processes in the most dramatic manner are likely to be those which are called upon to maintain the repression of the most threatening impulses or emotions.

The structure of character is not immediately apparent. It may be studied quite effectively, however, as it is manifested in the course of a person's life and in narrative accounts about life experiences. Let us return to Sherry's life narrative to examine the extent to which her decision may be understood by reference to the context of character.

In our first interview, she told her "life story in a nutshell" as follows:

> I'm Sherry O'Hearn. I'm 27 years old. My parents are Irish citizens and I'm first generation born in this country. My grandfather used to tell us that our ancestors go all the way back to Queen Anne Boleyn, but I don't know how true it is. So, I went to school, got married when I was 15, kept going to school, and got divorced from my husband three years ago. I work at a Ford plant. I'm an inspector, but because of my mechanical skills, they have me going around fixing machines [mumbles]. I got laid off after I had got my ninety days in. Now that I have my job back, I'm just sort of an extra person on inspection and my boss keeps giving me different kinds of jobs. It's a weird set-up because I don't know what I'm going to do when I go in. Today I went in to work and got sent home right away. So it's sort of a neat position to be in because it's something different every day . . . .
>
> My car got stolen a month ago. The first car I was ever able to buy got stolen. So I live a weird life.

Why do you think so?

Oh, kinda I do and kinda I don't. I'm independent and dependent at the same time. A lot of weird things just happen to me. I was in a bank once when it got robbed. I was down in the park where the kids hung out back in 1969 when the whole place got busted. They arrested everybody but me. The person who was sitting next to me went to prison and ended up getting beat up, but they missed me. They didn't even take me in. They just walked right past me. So a lot of weird things happen. I just happen to be there at the right time.

Sherry's self-presentation seems designed to emphasize her importance in a world which has not made her feel particularly significant. Her Irish heritage sets her apart, as does her possible genetic link to royalty. Since we already know that her husband dropped her for another woman, we may make sense of Sherry's identification with the rejected Ann Boleyn as another symbol of her rejection from some preferred state. The "weirdness" of Sherry's life seems to derive from her sensitivity to real and imagined rejections and losses. Her car is stolen. Her husband leaves her. She gets laid off. She is frequently unneeded at the factory. She even seems to regret being left out in the police raid on the park.

The feeling of being left out and an associated desire to displace another person are not restricted to Sherry's adult experience. As she retrospects, the theme finds expression repeatedly. We see both sides of the paradigm in one of her few memories from early childhood:

If you go way back to the earliest things you can remember, what would you say is the earliest memory?

I was about three. My dad had to get his teeth and his tonsils taken out all at the same time . . . and I remember taking soup into my dad and trying to feed him and spilling it down him. He was very tolerant of me. I remember watching my ma feeding my cousin some stuff like that, but I made such a mess, my ma would have to come in and shoo me out. "Let your dad eat by himself!"

I remember my mother being pregnant at that point. I used to get mad because when I would lie on her lap, the baby would kick me through her stomach. I used to hit her stomach and say, "That stupid baby . . ." and my mom says, "Well, it's gonna be your new baby brother or sister." I'd go, "Well, when he gets out, he's really gonna get it!" Then I remember my brother coming. . . . Oh, I loved my little brother. I always used to want to diaper him. I crawled into the crib one time when he was about a year old to change his diaper.

When I was getting out of the crib to get another diaper, he took the poop and rubbed it onto the wall. We got in so much trouble!

Early memories can be interpreted as symbols of prominent self-and-other representations (Mayman, 1968). In these memories, particularly in their sequence, we see a common childhood paradigm in play. Daughter temporarily displaces mother from her place with father. Daughter is ineffective and unable to maintain her position. Mother comes in to resume her rightful place. Another displacement occurs when Sherry's little brother comes on the scene. Her initial anger contributes to the exaggerated love she feels toward him. Again, she fails to do well in her role as little mother, gets herself in trouble, feels like she makes a mess of everything. In each case, she feels like an outsider and wants to be at the center of things.

Next we see a partial reversal of this theme in Sherry's account of a few summers she spent in Ireland during elementary school. Twice in our interviews I asked Sherry to recount highpoints in her life. Each time she referred to her stays in Ireland. Apparently, these were times when she felt special, wanted, and loved, but which also reproduced the rivalry we found in her earliest memories.

One of the major highpoints in my life was that my grandfather who passed away recently left me the property in Ireland. And one of the reasons he left it to me, instead of one of the boys is that I'm the only girl that was born to the second generation. So, I've got all boy cousins. So it comes down that everybody battled grandfather to get the property. The reason he gave it to me as it's stated in the will is because he used to take me there when I was younger and we used to go riding on the moors. If you've ever been to Ireland, it's real eerie type country because the moors just belch up this steam. It's just really eerie and I used to go horseback riding with him. At first snowfall, I spent a lot of time at my grandpa's. He'd come and get me out of bed and we'd make angels and my grandmother would stand up there yelling down at us, "You idiot, you get her in the house." Then we'd come in and grandma would come down. She's really tiny, she's only 4'11", and he was a man of about 6'4", and she'd be shaking her finger at him as she's making hot chocolate and bitchin' at him, feeding us hot chocolate and cookies.

Here is a second telling from another interview:

My grandfather was in love with first snowfalls. If it was a first snowfall, he'd come home and his hands would be all cold from the snow, and he'd wake me up and tell me to get my snow suit on and he'd take me outside in the middle of the darkness and the first snowfall.

I can remember him falling back and making angels in the snow, and I can remember my grandmother opening up the upstairs window and yelling, "Get that child back in here right now!" She'd come down and be boiling mad, you could just see the steam kind of poppin' off her head; she'd be standin' there bitchin' the whole time grandpa was takin' off my boots and everything – makin' hot chocolate.

Following each of these accounts, Sherry slipped into memories of difficult times with her parents: bruises from spankings, disagreements about how she should raise her own children, and a general defiance in the face of their authority.

What makes these memories the highpoints in Sherry's life? Speculation suggests the following possibilities, which could be confirmed or discarded through further inquiry. In these scenes, Sherry is able to please the grandfather, the big man. She has failed to do this in numerous other instances. Eros is bubbling on these misty rides through the moors and is neatly symbolized in the figure of the fallen angels on the virgin snow. The claim of the older woman, in this case, is not threatening, in fact, it is meant in jest and accompanied by nourishment.

Even without going into speculations about characteristic defenses which might underlie the themes which recur in Sherry's life narrative, we can safely specify a constellation of concerns which are currently salient. One of these is to have what men have, whether it be property, status, assertiveness, independence, or, more unconsciously, the attention and admiration of her mother. A related thematic concern is that a woman will stand between her and the man she wants to be close to, that she will prove inadequate to the point that she must be replaced. More broadly, there is a wish to be attended to, by anyone, and to feel important to someone. We can wonder if Sherry felt unwanted by her parents, for example, when they shipped her off to Ireland so often.

In conjunction with these concerns, assuming that they are rooted in early childhood experience, we would expect to find wishes to displace the mother, to win over the father, to get mother back, to get rid of the brother – all of which have apparently become associated with a quantum of anxiety, as they are strictly forbidden. Psychoanalytic theory informs us, with compelling evidence, that unacceptable wishes are excommunicated from consciousness by repression. Even symbols or images of their gratification are taboo. Symbols normally have the function of delaying and guiding action as urges are played out in fantasy, but when impulses are strictly forbidden, a "desymbolization" relegates them to an unconscious status (Lorenzer, 1976). The unconscious counterpart of a symbol may be referred to as a "stereotype." (This is definitely not to be confused with the common usage.) Roughly speaking, a stereotype is composed of a repressed intention, affectively charged, linking the self and an other. The fact that it is unconscious makes it affect behavior in an automatic way, much as imprinting dominates the behavior of certain animal species. A stereotype is thus resistant to conscious acknowledgement but has a particularly powerful meaning due to its relation to frustrated primary needs.

Stereotypes find expression in dreams, daydreams, and in action, but only on condition that a "scene" in which they can be played out is set up in fantasy or by real situations. On the basis of a number of narratives like Sherry's, one begins to realize that *when indecision is prolonged, the insistence of a stereotype is often required to bring it to an end.* Whenever one hears, for example, the expression, "That was the last straw!", it is more than likely that the elements of a stereotype are bearing down on the course of consciousness. This may sound mechanical, but as we proceed it will be clear that these "operations" are of a symbolic nature, relying on metaphorical relations.

Sherry's account of the events that brought about her divorce provides a glimpse of how this process unfolds. Sherry married Tom when she was 15 and Tom was 25. (It is no coincidence that her beloved grandfather was ten years older than his wife.) Although Tom was fairly well-off, he went to extremes in providing for Sherry and himself. On two occasions, he spent at least two years in jail for theft and robbery. She seems not to have minded these separations. As far as she is concerned, the problems in the marriage began when she got pregnant. Tom was enraged because he had been led to understand that due to an accident she suffered as a teenager, Sherry would be unable to have children. He started "running around" with another woman, Suzie. Sherry found out about Suzie in a manner which neatly fitted the pattern of her childhood recollections:

We moved into a new house after I had my second child. We were invited to a party at the end of October. Tom asked Suzie to go and he asked me to go and he had forgotten that he had asked both of us to go. Well, it ended up being a really big scene and it really flipped me out because Tom came up to me pointing to a friend of mine and said,

"Hey, that's my girlfriend and if you don't like it, tough shit." Well, this just shattered me. I didn't know how to cope with it, so I did the proverbial number of threatening suicide to the point that I did cut my wrist and I did bleed a little bit, but I didn't die. I was too chicken to take sleeping pills. I had two little babies, so I wasn't going to do anything that bad.

Having failed to get rid of herself, Sherry tried to give her children to an orphanage – a sign that what she had just experienced recreated some feeling that had primarily to do with her own childhood. Following this event, Sherry took a trip to visit a very nurturant couple in another state, then came back and put Tom out of the house. At this point, too, the change becomes an issue of childhood dependency versus adult autonomy.

What kind of things were you thinking while you were on that trip?

First I had to decide that I was intelligent enough to make it on my own. I was a big girl and I didn't need the help of my mommy and daddy. You always need their help, but I didn't need to rely on them as heavily. It was like standing in front of the mirror and saying, "Hey, you're a big kid now. Time to grow up."

And, in another interview, she sees the decision in similar terms:

It was just a matter of getting my shit together. . . . It taught me to rely on myself. Before that I always had my parents and Tom was there, too.

The links that Sherry establishes between her need to be independent and separating from her parents and Tom are important insights. Anyone would be upset by the incident at the party, but Sherry is doubly bothered by it because it resonates thematically with the displacement she seems to have experienced as a child. Forced to survive on her own and hurt by rejection, even feeling cut off to the point of trying to cut off her own life, she pushed herself to "grow up" and denied her ungratified yearnings to be dependent.

In the light of the notions of character and stereotype developed here, it is finally possible to comprehend at least one major facet of Sherry's decision to have the affair with Carl. We were puzzled by the apparent contradiction between Sherry's conscious deliberation and her eventual decision, as well as the curious "the more I thought about it, the better idea it seemed" phenomenon. The evidence implies that as Sherry remembered the pain of her divorce, considered the consequences it had for her life, dwelled on the public embarrassment she underwent, these memories lined up, so to speak, with the childhood paradigms described earlier. The energy to enact the scene in its victorious version collected in that process. The thematic similarity between distant past, recent past, and present scenes lies not only in common emotional states (anger, disappointment, shame) but also in the positions taken up by the "actors." Father (Tom-Carl) and mother (Suzie-Carl's wife) may or may not give up their own togetherness to let little Sherry in. As Sherry considers the more recent situation with Tom and Suzie, the earliest layers of the stereotype reverberate simultaneously. We may speculate that the "hate" directed at Suzie, which is so quickly denied, draws its energy from the unacknowledgeable rage Sherry harbors toward her mother. (Their quarrels and conflicts are dominant topics throughout the interviews.)

It turns out that Carl has a number of features which may have contributed to Sherry's ability to overcome both her vow not to date married men and her moral training. Carl is bearded like her grandfather, is short in stature and of temper like her funny grandmother (even jumps up and down when angry), and is the spitting image of her favorite singer. To top it off, Carl holds the same position and has the same aims in the factory as did Sherry's father and has the same striking hair color for which Sherry envies her mother.

The essence of *rationalization* and its role in decision making is clarified in the passage above. Rationalization is commonly understood as the justification of an action on grounds other than its primary motives. It is an intellectualizing defense which maintains repression of an unacceptable wish. The possibility of coming to a decision, not that one would always want to decide, is enhanced by rationalization because certain actual feelings can be denied outright: "It's not that I hated Suzie . . ." and the situation can be construed in a manner that minimizes conflict about moving into it: "It's not my fault that he's going out on his wife." Sherry's insistence that this was a "big decision" that took her a long time to make obscures the sense she must have had at first (I'm guessing at this on the basis of the coincidences just listed) that she would not be able to resist Carl's offer.

Stereotyped action is rationalized by calling it a decision, a term which implies the exercise of reason and logical thought.

A final excerpt from these fascinating interviews with Sherry should clinch the argument that the power of stereotypes is not to be minimized.

Carl gave Sherry tickets to a Halloween party (at the end of October, just like the party fiasco with Tom) to which he had also invited his wife. Sherry dressed up as a black cat. (Poe's story, "The Black Cat,"

with which she is quite familiar, being a lover of Poe's work, is about a
cat which gives away the carefully concealed murder of a woman by her
alcoholic husband.) Sherry's costume won second place that night.
Ironically, Carl's wife argued with the judges that Sherry should have
been awarded first place.

The repetition of the scene in this case required a number of external
manipulations over which Sherry had no control, but the tone in which
she recounted this tale was definitely one of gleeful mischievousness
and happy revenge.

What are the implications of this perspective on choice? First, it is
clear that the impact of character on decision making arises largely
from the fact that a person's self-understanding is conditioned in a set
of social relations or interaction paradigms of a very limited range.
Parents are likely to take up only a few, but perhaps inconsistent,
stances toward a child, thus interacting with him/her in ways which
institute a particular, specifiable self-concept and a related unconscious
defensive structure. Problems in deciding may prove to stem from
conflicting interaction paradigms (e.g., between what mother and
father would want), from seeking aims expressing unacceptable wishes
(hostile, incestuous, envious, etc.), or from conflicts between social
norms and personal inclination.

Second, every concern or interest adopted by an individual is much
more than a private choice. It is grounded in conscious or unconscious
images of self in relation to others. The isolated prospector searching
for gold has his poor family in mind. The child discovering a leaf runs
to a parent in glee. The scientist imagines the respect of his colleagues
and the people his discoveries will help. We forget that our everyday
concerns are saturated with the lessons of socialization and that our
daily habits are performed as much with or apart from an other as for
oneself. Our views of reality are originally constructed on the foundations of interpersonal experience. It is in interactions with others
that we come to value one realm of life more than another – sports
more than religion, money more than education, guns more than skis,
music more than visual arts, and so on.

Even the more intelligent among us try to deny this, perhaps in a
claim to originality or individuality. I was particularly struck by this
passage in the autobiography of Herbert Read, an English novelist,
where he tries to prove that his interest in reading and writing had no
basis in social interaction:

> I had already discovered the joy of reading – had, indeed, brought it
> with me to school. This predilection I believe to have been innate

. . . I try now (as I did in another work) to recollect any influence in my boyhood which might have encouraged this latent tendency. There is none. This taste was self-evident, and I persisted in it against all sorts of obstacles.

Such an innate taste of reading, which is merely the vicarious exercise of imagination, is fairly common among boys; what I next discovered in myself, though I did not at that time attach any significance to it, was a taste for writing.   (Read, 1963, p. 152)

He admits that there were some encouragements to his writing while he was in school,

But I insist that the impulse to write, the love of words for their own sake and for the sake of what they could express, was precedent, and no more to be explained by personal influences than the colour of my hair or the pitch of my voice.   (Read, 1963, p. 153)

The tendency to deny the social-relational ground of our desires and goals is a manifestation of the constraining impact of self-and-other-images in the everyday wanderings of consciousness. The world is set up as a mirror in which the self can regard itself, imagining its own appearance as others perceive it. This alienation of consciousness as it seeks recognition in the mirror held up by others is the basis for a stable sense of identity and purpose, but also constitutes the possibility for transformations of that sense because experience in social relations is hardly uniform. Each "other" has different expectations. As a result, our identities are so riddled with contradictions that many changes in life are brought about merely in attempts to resolve issues stemming from those contrasting relationships.

A final implication of our analysis of Sherry's narrative is that while the context of character as viewed from a life history perspective is far from being the only one, it is already clear that the Freudian dictum that human behavior is *over*determined – always flows from multiple sources – is no exaggeration. As we examine other contexts, it will become increasingly absurd to imagine that a decision has a single reason. One cannot justifiably claim, "I am going to do this because. . . ." In fact, that common reason, "because I *want* to," comes close to being a good answer. Unraveling the meaning of a decision can be a frustrating experience precisely because of this overdetermination. The ground keeps slipping away. Yet, self-understanding apparently proceeds on the basis of such self-questioning. One can at least get closer to knowing what one wants and why one wants it.

QUESTIONS ABOUT DECIDING: THE PRACTICAL CONTEXT

Other than the context of character, what else begs to be considered in an adequate psychology of decision making? What impinges so directly on the course of deliberation that it must never be ignored?

It is tempting to reply: *everything*, the entire world – history, society, culture.

Yet, for a given individual, only specific aspects of the totality bear directly on decisions. A specific history, a particular society and culture. Once I assumed that within the homogeneous culture of post-industrial society we were all up against pretty much the same issues and problems. (My studies in psychology had done little to undermine this illusion.) One interview in particular forced me to open my eyes a bit wider. That interview will serve quite well to introduce a framework for the consideration of the other contexts of choice, and against which the various theories of decision making – visions of decisions – may be tested.

I had advertised for volunteers in a working-class community newspaper. I knew I had a good sense of how upper-middle-class young adults made decisions (I had worked at a prestigious university counseling center for two years). It was time to develop contacts with other subcultures. The ad read: Researcher would like to record your life history and discuss important decisions you have made. Two women replied, each of them saying she had a "real story to tell." Both of the stories turned out to be painful accounts of hard times. They both thought I must be in the business of ghost-writing auto-biographies. Their visions of easy money faded as I explained my project, but they agreed to help me out.

Mary, the respondent whose interview is excerpted here at length, told me that she was "sort of married," had two kids, and that her current big decision was to sue the company that had recently fired her. I knew already that this woman would teach me something I could not have learned from students worrying whether to major in business or history, or deciding where to go for graduate school.

On the day of the appointment, I drove past a long row of industrial plants and warehouses, car junkyards, and gravel pits bordering the apartment complex where Mary lived. Her building, although not more than ten to fifteen years old, was quite run down. Dog feces and torn newssheets littered the common hallway. I waited a couple of minutes after ringing the bell. The door finally opened. Mary had sent her 6-year old to see who it was. Momentarily, Mary emerged in a robe from the bedroom. She looked very tired, pale, and disheveled: "Oh, yeah, you were the one who wanted to interview me." She sat nervously across from me while I explained my project again and led in with this question:

You said you had wanted to write your life story. Could you tell me what you would say? How would you start?

Can I go back to when I first got married?

As far as you want.

I'm embarrassed. [Laughs] You know what's really strange is that most of what I've gone through in my life is nothing but calling the police, *deciding whether or not to put abusive men in jail.* Okay? . . . for abusing kids . . . um . . . and being put into a situation that you just can't get out of. That's where I'll start.

Seven years ago I got married, and this guy had *money.* . . . It wasn't a poverty situation, and everybody says, "Don't leave, because you've got a house, you've got lots of cars, and you've got lots of money," and I said, "No, I don't want that because it doesn't take the place of being happy." So after I got out of that mess I got into another one where I'm rehabilitating a baby [laughs] and I had to support him for about three years. That's when I got my job at the supermarket and *they* fired me because I wasn't one of the family. I don't know what else you want to know!

Mary's disjointed story, reflecting the pummeling life had recently dished out, stunned me and pushed me into a more directive interviewing stance than I care to adopt. She seemed to be asking for someone to make sense of it for her.

What were things like before you got married? What stands out?

Nothing. Because all that's in my mind now. [Her 2-year old interrupts] I can't even go back to my childhood because it's been *battered*. It's just gone. I can't explain; it's like I don't remember any of those happy days. It's like once in a great while, if I was shopping in a grocery store [clears throat] maybe my dad would say, "Here, kids. This buggy's for you. Go put what you want in it." And I'll flash back . . . because now it's me and I'm maybe with this rotten guy that's saying "Hey, no, your kids can't have this because it costs $1.17 and we need that for a bottle of beer, so forget it." That's the type of situation it is. So it's a complete *knockout* of every good memory you've had in your past. Because as far as childhood memories, I don't really have any. . . . And that's bad because I had a good family. I still do. I was never brought up that way. It's just the mess you get into. And if you're not that strong. . . .

I had unwittingly steered her away from discussing the phase of her life in which she had been abused, yet her vocabulary insists that violence is *the* issue. Her choices in the present are subject to an order of force. The issues are no longer psychological, yet our culture's individualism inclines us to look inside for solutions to our problems, as Mary's narrative demonstrates:

I've been to a psychiatrist. I've taken my kids to them and they don't even tell you which way to go. They help you to see different routes to take, but they'll never say "Yes, you should do this; you should get out of this mess," or a yes-or-no type deal where they actually tell you what to do with your life. . . . It's something *you* gotta decide, you know?"

Would you really want them to tell you what to do?

Yeah, I wish they could have told me what to do, because I would have did it a long time ago and would have been a lot happier for it. Like the first time it took me three years to get out of such a bad marriage. This time I can't even *afford* to do that, to get help, you know, somebody to say this way or that way.

Can you remember what it was like when you were deciding to get into that first marriage? How old were you then?

Seventeen, my first child was born when I was 18.

What did you like about this person?

Security. Mostly security. You know, I could walk down the street without worrying about him letting somebody beat me up. [Laughs] Also for financial security. I had never worked a day in my life before I met him. I was just out of high school. In fact, I had him talk me into getting out of high school in the 11th grade, into quitting high school when I had always wanted to graduate. He said there was too many guys there and if I didn't quit we wouldn't get married. So I quit and I ended up going to night school and there were millions more guys there. So it was just as bad, but we ended up getting married anyhow. . . . A lot of it was out of fear, though, because he used to . . . he . . . stroked me many times before we were married, but I . . . and then after that I figured, "Well, I better marry this guy now," because by that time all the plans were made, the halls were rented, the church, the band. In fact, we called it off. I called it off, you know, but then it was on again a month later. So I knew back in my mind that maybe I shouldn't do this, but at the time I was just stuck and "God, I can't put everybody through this!" . . . You know, "Everybody had a couple of showers and I just better do it, . . . What are all the people gonna say?" So that's when I just went through with it.

Sensing my interest in her first decision to marry, Mary tries to explain the circumstances that led her down the aisle despite the fact that she had already been beaten by her intended husband. A number of factors combined to leave her no acceptable way out. Her friends tell her that the man's money will bring a new life. She would be too embarrassed to give back all the presents she had received at showers. Perhaps most importantly, an aspect she leaves unsaid, she must have been afraid of what he would do to her if she refused to go through with the wedding.

Mary left her husband for a while after some months of marriage. The abuse had not stopped. Then she discovered she was pregnant, and although she says she really did not want the child, she returned to her husband, delivered, and stayed in miserable circumstances for three more years. When her best friends started threatening to have her child taken away – Mary saw this as a betrayal – she began to consider divorce. Again, the *practical* aspects of her situation made that option difficult to consider. This is how she reconstructs her deliberation at that point:

> I knew that I had better make a move out, but I could not leave. I had to decide. I had my own house. God, I had anything a woman would want, all right? How was I going to go on? I just got out of school. I never had worked a day in my life, right? How was I gonna make my house payments? How was I gonna be the man? I didn't want to do all that, so I just gave it up and went back to my ma's to start all over again. It was the only way I could forget all that I went through in those three years.

Then the painful cycle began again, due to fairly similar conditions:

> I was at my mom's for about a year. I was living there really good and was saving a lot of money. I got hired at a supermarket and then I went to a bar and met this nerd. [Laughs] No, I met this really nice guy that really had a lot of money again. He had no problems. Well, everybody's got problems, but I was still very naive to the whole outside world. You figure from 17 to 20, I was in a little cage and I broke out; so this guy *did* fool me. He was an ex-drug addict. He never told me that. He never told me a lot of things. I found out these things later on, on my own. He talked me into moving in with him so we rented a place and I moved in and married him three months later, so I could get out of my mom's because with the baby, it was causing a little bit of a hassle.
>
> I was married within a year after my divorce. On top of the drug problem I found out he was an alcoholic. But I felt sorry for him, so I stayed in and kept trying to rehabilitate him. He would tell me it was because his mother committed suicide four years before, so that was always an excuse for the drinking. It was because his mom died, or because there wasn't enough money. He used it all for getting his buzz.
>
> After that we lost a couple of places we were living in, so we just kept on moving. So I just ended up throwing him out and filed for divorce again. It kind of straightened him out for about seven months. But if that doesn't work, it's gonna have to be jail.
>
> And that's gonna take a lot of courage, because I'm worried that if I do put him behind bars for assault and battery . . . no human being deserves to be hit, I don't care what anybody says . . . that if I put him behind bars maybe it will show him. But if I put him behind bars, when he gets out, he may come after me again. [Laughs] See, I

don't want to do that either. So, I don't really know where I'm going to go and that's kind of where I'm standing right now.

At this point we may pose a number of questions that an adequate perspective on decision making must help us to answer. Many readers will be inclined to ask questions bearing on character and the life history: Why did Mary go ahead with her first wedding even though her fiancé was beating her? We might say that social pressure against canceling the wedding was a factor, but certainly the general social consensus would be against marrying a man who beats his girlfriend. Mary chose to let social pressure and potential embarrassment outweigh her doubts about her fiancé. Is she subject to an urge to act against her interests? Is this a case of masochism, pure and simple? Does she get some perverse pleasure out of abuse? Is Mary trying to work through some unconscious sense of guilt by setting herself up for punishment?

To accept the above considerations as primary in understanding Mary's choices would border on theoretical sadism. The constraints of objective conditions far outweigh those imposed by her character. Her character itself must be viewed as the result of extended involvement in oppressive objective conditions.

The approach which analyzes practical facts of everyday life as they impinge on decisions may be referred to as a *life-structural* perspective. It offers the most comprehensive basis for understanding the practical context of choice.

Daniel Levinson, in *The Seasons of a Man's Life* (1978), introduces the concept of the "life structure" as a framework for grasping the multifaceted development of a person's life. The life structure is a global concept referring to the *current* psychosocial totality of an individual. It encompasses not only overt behavior, but also unexpressed longings, moods, regrets, and attitudes about one's life, as well as the referents of these activities and feelings.

A life structure is "the underlying pattern or design of a person's life at any given time" (p. 41). To understand a life structure, three overlapping perspectives are necessary. The first attends to immediate involvements in relationships and roles, called "self-world transactions." The second perspective examines the degree to which individual potential is realized given the constraints and opportunities of a particular set of activities. Levinson lists skills, goals, wishes, ideals, fantasies, and conflicts in this realm. Finally, one can look at the mediations between a person's activities and their sociocultural contexts – social movements, economic trends, political events, public attitudes, technological developments, and class position.

Because it has *regular* components, some of which are looked forward to and others which are anticipated with disgust, everyday life comes to be experienced as a *structure*. It is also a structure in the sense that it is imposed from without by cultural codes, job requirements, role expectations, and the like. It is simultaneously conditioned from within (in a manner of compromise with external factors) by self-images and unconscious intentions.

From a life-structural perspective, Mary's decisions could be viewed as distinctly related to economic or financial aspects of her situation. Both of the men she found attractive had appealing incomes. She could end her dependence on her relatively poor parents by moving out into the world, attain adult status, enjoy the material comforts of advanced industrial society, and fulfill the maternal role she was apparently socialized to interpret as a personal requirement. Similarly, her life is constrained currently by financial problems: limited income, debts, lack of capital. As she seeks to be a good mother and wife, she is definitely hindered by sheer material obstacles which, regardless of psychological traits, are difficult to overcome, particularly for someone who has been deprived of skills by an ineffective public education system.

Exclusive reference to economic factors, however, is not sufficient to enlighten us about the persistence of Mary's inclination to choose abusive men. This problem, referred to in Freudian literature as the "compulsion to repeat", is definitely a phenomenon to be understood as we consider self-misunderstanding in major life decisions. If we stand back from the point of view which regards Mary's dilemma as resulting from her character, as a matter for psychology, and simultaneously suspend the life-structural account in which we have already dabbled, it becomes clear that our question about deciding will need to relate those two conceptual realms to each other. It appears that Mary's social environment and economic situation provide a scene for the enactment of psychologically grounded tendencies, even while those tendencies may have been encouraged by her involvement in that social nexus. Other people enter into the decisions she has made; she is not entirely alone. Those decisions derive their *impetus* and *significance* from the social and material relations they attempt to mediate.

If we return to Mary's account to see how she is thinking about her current situation, we will be in a position to organize our concepts of life history and life structure more coherently.

Mary was fired from her job as a cashier when a few lottery tickets were found missing. She was accused of stealing them. The union chose not to defend her. Mary thinks the union representatives were bought out by the supermarket. ''I was a habitual grievance writer. I had paid my dues and fees, but they didn't like me to write grievances. I didn't let them get away with nothing.''

Mary is now on welfare and is separated from her husband. He refuses to give her a divorce. She has told him that if he straightens up he can come home for Christmas, but she would prefer him not to do that: ''Last year he smashed up some of the children's presents. When do you believe that someone has changed? When do you know if they are telling the truth?'' So, what is Mary planning to do? How does she think about her situation?

Right now, I'm trying to get my job back. I would like to sue the whole company, because if I got my job back they would fire me again. Even if I went to another store, the manager who gave me trouble would transfer through the chain and end up supervising me again. He would fire me and I would lose my house. I've already lost my credit. I made enough money at bingo to pay off my loans, but they wouldn't give me a new loan for a washing machine. They could take my money for two years, but couldn't lend me any more.

What is the best future that you can imagine?

I have talked to eight lawyers and maybe I'll be rich someday. [Laughs] I will win my lawsuit and I'm gonna burn them for so much money I'll probably own the chain. That's really how I feel. I'm going to tell them who I'm gonna hire and fire.

What would you do with that money?

Probably go buy my old house back. I really regret letting my first husband buy me out. He paid me $4,000 for the house, property in Georgia, cars, and tons of furniture. I never wanted to give up my house, but I had no way of keeping it. Now when I look back, I see I could have gone on welfare. But I never knew . . . and of course I thought maybe he would come over and bomb it. So I thought I better just get out of it.

As far as the future, I don't know if I am going to win my case, but with eight different attorneys looking at it, listening to what I've got to say. . . . It will be a big fight, because I'm the little guy and they're the big people, right? But I know I'm gonna win. I really just want my job back and to be left alone, but if they're gonna play like this and let my kids suffer. . . .

Mary continues, reproducing the interior monologue she apparently
runs through frequently as she seeks a workable stance toward the
future.

So now I think, should I take my job back? Maybe that way they'll
give me some back pay. They would owe that to any human
being. . . . But, like I say, they'll just boot me out in two years
again. And by then maybe I'll have a house or a car and maybe I'd
lose it all again. I don't want that to happen, so maybe I'll get them to
give me enough cash to cover it all. Then I'll feel secure . . . you
know?

What's the worst future you can imagine?

Staying right where I'm at. It's going no place. You figure you're
getting older. I started out at 17 and now [counts] eight years later, I
have lost. I have gone down the ladder, instead of up. I mean I have
lost. And when I was by myself, I *gained*. If I *have* to I'll just be by
myself again, so I can crawl right back up that ladder. My old man
when he was here, my husband, he did not want me to go to school;
he did not want me to do anything, because . . . I don't know, he
didn't want me to progress or be better than I might have been at the
time.

My mom and dad have been with me through all this. But now my
dad's ready to retire. He has a lot of health problems. He has worked
all his life. In fact, he never even took vacations, because he was a
hard worker. Nowadays nobody really wants to work to make their
money. I'd like to be back there [live at home] and help him out,
but. . . .

Why couldn't you?

Well, I could, but I've got two kids. My ma is pretty sick. I don't
think her nerves could really handle it. But, there's my dad sitting
with no money after he has bailed me out millions of times – every
four or five months I'm just about being evicted, because when my
husband was living here he would not pay the rent. He knew
somebody else would help out. Then my husband's father would get
him his job back at the shop every four months. It was like a big
circle.

Like I said, I'd like to go back home and just help my dad out, but I
don't think I can do that. On the other hand, I'd have to come up with
another $1,000 sum, just to get moved into another place on my own
when I do get ready to move back out. I'm afraid if I do that I'll fall

into a trap of meeting another guy to live with and find out he's an ex-junkie and an alcoholic and God-knows-what nowadays. I find many people don't even want to work anymore . . . and it's the good people who get hurt.

I never went to college. I didn't need to go to college. Nobody had to teach me, because I learned it through experiencing it. Life teaches you. You can't read any book that will tell you any more. You can't learn it unless you live through it.

What exactly have you learned about life?

From my eyes, it's about being *fooled* . . . you really have to know what you are doing all the time. That's all I can say, you know, you can get fooled so easy. . . .

I feel I'm beginning to stand up for myself. I can imagine all the other women who must be in my shoes that can't. Imagine what they do when they're being beat so bad, and people say: "Why don't you run out or call the police?" I've seen that phone pulled off the wall so many times. There's no way you can get out of the house. There's no way you can call, no way to do anything but take what's happening to you. And after it's happened to you, if you've still got energy to walk and move, then you go and call. And you're still afraid. I've thought of going to take karate lessons in case I run into somebody like this again. Then if anybody really tried to put it over on me, I'd really give it to 'em.

How do you make sense of men being this way? You seem to expect to run into others.

It's all that I have seen. I've only seen two men be like this to me, and I have good memories of my father and I've got a brother who is a good worker. Neither of them hit their wives. I've talked to a lot of married couples and I've asked them, "Hey, do you hit your wife?" The first thing that comes out of my mouth is, "Do you hit women?" They say "No" and I sit and wonder if they really do to their wives what mine does behind closed doors. I can look back and say, "My father never did this. Why should I let this guy do this." Some girls have gotten out of it, after their husband threw them in a ditch and hit them on the back. But where do I get the strength? You know what I mean? When is my time finally going to come around and I'll say "Hey, I'm sick of this." Maybe when I'm financially set I can say, "I don't need to stick with this freak, or let my kids grow up seeing this kind of stuff."

It came to where I even talked to this priest. After a while you see that nothing is working and you're gonna have to start praying. He told me, "You, there's something wrong with you. You feel you have to be punished. Something you did years ago makes you feel like you have to take this kind of treatment from men." Or else, I find somebody that I have to rehabilitate. Every person I'm wrong with, I'm attracted to.

What is eventually going to happen is as soon as my kids are a little older and I can stand on my own two feet, I'm going to have to break away from my husband, just for my kids. . . . I've got to come to some conclusion. [Laughs] Something's gonna finally break and I'm gonna make a move, and it's gonna have to be pretty soon. I don't know whether it will be because my daughter's father is trying to take her away from me, or my best friend turning us in for child abuse, or my sister who looks at me and says, "I'm gonna get those kids taken away from you if you don't get them out of there." My kids talk. They say what's going on. It doesn't even have to be me. *Then* I know it is getting serious. To put my kids first will help me, too, to decide whether to go through with the divorce or just throw him out. Who goes first? Him, my kids, or me? How do you figure out who really needs the help the most? It's tough.

Mary continues discussing details about her current husband and his problems. Then she reasserts her desire to move back home to take care of her ailing father, but again cancels that wish by assuming that her children would bother her parents too much.

An analysis of this section of the transcript raises a number of questions which overlap our earlier ones and about which we would hope to be enlightened by a psychology of decision making. Our progress is hindered slightly by the fact that Mary sees herself as making up her mind about at least two interconnected issues. The first regards the matter of getting a second divorce and the second has to do with how to get her job back or at least retaliate against the company that fired her or the union that failed to support her. We will focus later on the latter issue, but Mary has made and is making a variety of decisions, about which we need to understand at least the following:

1   the determinants of the course of deliberation (Why does Mary alternate between an assertive stance and a passive one? Between optimism and pessimism?)
2   the inability to decide (What prevents Mary from listening to herself, from acting now to change her circumstances? What will it take to get her over the threshold?)
3   the role of character in decision making (Is Mary prevented from

returning home by "Oedipal" strivings? She seems drawn to her father but sees her mother as not able to tolerate her presence. Is there something about Mary's habitual attitude or stance toward life that sets her up to be "fooled"?)

4 the problem of rationalization (Mary wants to ignore evidence that most other women are not beaten by their husbands and sounds as if she would put up with it if it were the norm. It seems that she tries to rationalize her situation in order not to make a decision. In other words, she construes her world in a manner serving to prevent the need to move or make a change. She thinks it will take some force from outside herself to force a move.)

5 the sense of knowing that neither the best nor the worst imaginable futures are likely, but not being able to act in terms of realistic perceptions of one's situation – in short, the problem of authenticity (Mary senses that when her kids are a little older and she is on her feet financially she will break away from her husband. Knowing this, why isn't she now filing for a divorce, i.e. acting in conjunction with her actual intentions?)

6 the constitution of alternatives (possibilities) and the manner in which they came to be considered feasible or impractical (How does Mary come to be considering the alternatives she does – suing the company, moving back home, putting her husband in jail – and what social and psychological factors contribute to the appeal of one over the others?)

7 and, again, the problem of repetition (Mary indicates that she is likely to run into more abusive men, to lose her house again, to have people threatening to take away her children. What is the *meaning* of these fears? How will they affect her decisions?).

Several additional points need to be made here in anticipation of arguments to come.

Mary's decision to sue the company that fired her clearly can not be reduced to its practical intent. She tells us that it is a way of getting money to make up for past losses and to make her coming years more comfortable. But it also has a more deeply subjective sense. She tells us that it is a first sign of standing up for herself, a way of getting revenge, a moment of the perpetual big-guy-versus-little-guy struggle, and even (in a part of the transcript not presented) a way of trying to save her marriage. (Mary imagines that her husband would behave if they only had enough money to lead a comfortable life.)

Apart from Mary's self-understandings, we can also justifiably construe her decision as an action embedded in various *social* trends.

Among these, we could mention as examples the increased dependence on litigation as a means of resolving social conflict, the growing sympathies between unions and management, and the contribution of the media to the get-rich-quick mentality.

In another vein, Mary's decision could be viewed as a case of identification with the oppressor/aggressor (Freire, 1970; A. Freud, 1937). Especially when we consider her fantasies of buying the company and making personnel decisions herself, we can conclude that the meaning of this decision resides partially in the long history of domination which now structures Mary's intentions. Many, but not all, references to the life history should include an examination of unconscious desires that effect the life course.

Finally, this decision cannot be understood in isolation from the totality of Mary's current activities and involvements. The various unconnected activities which fill everyday life are in fact linked in numerous ways. Seemingly unrelated spheres of her life may have played an important role in bringing about this particular decision. For example, Mary's win at bingo may have convinced her that she is due for a run of good fortune, so she might as well take a chance with the lawsuit. Or perhaps there was a difficult confrontation with her parents recently, making Mary more desperate for solutions other than moving back home.

We are thus led to conclude that the contexts of deciding, while they can be roughly grouped into the life-historical and the life-structural, are multifaceted. Our only hope of developing a critical psychology of decision making lies in examining the various ways in which the context of choice mediate each other and, in so doing, influence the life course. Joseph Veroff (1983) recently proposed that personality can only be understood as an expression of interacting contexts: historical, cultural, developmental, organizational, and interpersonal. A similar extreme complexity obscures our vision of the processes of decision making. Indeed, when personality is construed in this broad manner, we come very close to the sort of understanding we will require in an adequate psychology of decision making.

AMERICAN PSYCHOLOGIES OF DECISION MAKING

The legacy of William James

The introspective approach of William James got American psychologies of decision making off to a great start. The chapter on "Will" in his *Principles of Psychology* (1890) offers an account of deciding which is one of the most riveting available. Somewhere along the line, however, the baton was not relayed. Both James' approach and his concrete descriptions were ignored in mainstream psychology in America for decades and were discovered afresh only recently in a new wave of interest.

A few key passages from James will convey the tone and texture of his perspective:

> We are now in a position to describe *what happens in deliberate action*, or when the mind is the seat of many ideas related to each other in antagonistic or in favorable ways. One of the ideas is that of an act. By itself this idea would prompt a movement; some of the additional considerations, however, which are present to consciousness block the motor discharge whilst others, on the contrary, solicit it to take place. The result is that peculiar feeling of inward unrest known as *indecision*. . . .

> The process of deliberation contains endless degrees of complication. At every moment of it our consciousness is of an extremely complex

object, namely the existence of the whole set of motives and their conflict. . . . Of this object, the totality of which is realized more or less dimly all the while, certain parts stand out more or less sharply at one moment in the foreground, and at another moment other parts, in consequence of the oscillations of our attention, and of the "associative" flow of our ideas. . . . The deliberation may last for weeks or months, occupying at intervals the mind. The motives which yesterday seemed full of urgency and blood and life today feel strangely weak and pale and dead. But as little today as tomorrow is the question finally resolved.   (James, 1890, pp. 528–9)

Deliberation, James continues, is impatient. It is prone to decide to "relieve the tensions of doubt and hesitancy. Thus it comes that we will often take any course whatever which happens to be most vividly before our minds, at the moment when this impulse to decisive action becomes extreme" (p. 530). This comment anticipates one of the more important "findings" to be had from our study of decisions as described in life narratives.

On the other hand, deliberation is sustained by a countermotive, a "dread of the irrevocable." Decisions, James points out, are not irrevocable, yet we seem to ignore this, preferring to be resolute and hating to change our minds.

By definition, deliberation ends when a decision is achieved. James notes (pp. 531–4) five ways this can happen. The first is the decision that is "reasonable." It arrives calmly, with a sense of freedom and lack of coercion. A feeling of rightness is achieved after a "rational balancing" of considerations renders a particular future obviously preferable. James clearly believes that the ideal decision is of this sort and that it is likely to be made by a certain type of person – an indication that he is sensitive to the impact of character on decision processes: "A 'reasonable' character is one who has a store of stable and worthy ends, and who does not decide about an action till he has calmly ascertained whether it be ministerial or detrimental to any of these" (p. 532).

The remaining types of decisions are deviations from this ideal. Types two and three follow the motto that "even a bad decision is better than no decision at all." The decision arrives as if by accident, determined either from without or by an inward, drifting impulse to be done with indecision. The latter type of decision is "too abrupt and tumultuous to occur often in humdrum and cool-blooded natures. But it is probably frequent in persons of strong emotional endowment and unstable or vacillating character" (p. 533).

The fourth type of decision arises from a change of attitude which forces "an instant abandonment of the more trivial projects with which we had been dallying, and an instant practical acceptance of the more grim and earnest alternative which till then could not extort our mind's consent" (p. 533). This is a decision which follows the feeling of having to "face the facts" or "get down to business."

The final type is of an entirely different order. Here, "we feel, in deciding, as if we ourselves by our own willful act inclined the beam" (p. 534) toward a certain alternative. This bears further description as it is commonly involved in major life decisions.

> The slow dead heave of the will that is felt in these instances makes them a class altogether different from all the three preceding classes. . . . Subjectively and phenomenally, the *feeling of effort*, absent from the former decisions accompanies these. Whether it be the dreary resignation for the sake of austere and naked duty of all sorts of rich mundane delights, or whether it be the heavy resolve that of two mutually exclusive trains of future fact, both sweet and good, and with no strictly objective or imperative principle of choice between them, one shall forevermore become impossible, while the other shall become a reality, it is a desolate and acrid sort of act, an excursion into a lonesome moral wilderness. . . . [H]ere both alternatives are steadily held in view, and in the very act of murdering the vanquished possibility the chooser realizes how much he is in that instant making himself lose. It is deliberately driving a thorn into one's flesh. . . .   (p. 534)

This is the sort of decision we are most concerned to understand, by which subjects I interviewed are most intrigued, and that most American decision theories since James have chosen to ignore. Even in James' account, the problem at hand in such decisions is too readily reduced to a pathology of the will. In a discussion of the explosive and the obstructed will, paralleling the modern categories of the impulsive and obsessive personalities, James argues that the effort required in the painful type of decision just described derives from the fact that these cases involve "ideal or moral action" winning out over sensual or practical resistance. Effort is required to concentrate *attention* on the image of that which one wills to become a reality. This can be painful because one also *cares* about other things that must be excluded, ignored, or given up in order to concentrate on the chosen end.

The onset of behaviorism in the 1920s largely overshadowed the introspective insights of the sort James put forward. Attempts to study scientifically only that which could be *observed* relegated decision making, along with a host of other fascinating subjective processes, to the "black box." This overcompensation for subjectivistic tendencies in psychology need not be seen as a total setback. It concentrated attention on the extent to which actions can be accounted, for by objective conditions, environmental factors, and the like. The power of consciousness in determining action is definitely limited. Psychoanalysis was demonstrating the same point from another angle while the behaviorists continued their attack.

The shape of the general psychology of decision making did not undergo much of a revolution, however, until much later. Woodworth's (1940, pp. 397–401) introductory text, for example, discusses a number of points which duplicate James' description. He tells us that decisions are called for when there is a conflict of motives; that the state of indecision is a complex activity in which a unity is sought; that a certain satisfaction is achieved through coming to a decision, partially compensating for the loss of excluded possibilities; that deliberation is rarely pursued to the "bitter end" for reasons of practicality; and that decisions do not always follow the stronger motive. The impact of psychoanalysis is clear in a conclusion that rejected motives may be deferred, repressed, and satisfied in modified forms (displacement).

Before the behavioristic paradigm broke in the face of criticism and became the "cognitive-behavioral" approach, the complexity of decision making was frequently reduced to an analysis of types of conflicts, namely the familiar approach-approach, approach-avoidance, and avoidance-avoidance conflicts. Lundin (1969, p. 304), for example, defines conflict as "the presentation of simultaneous stimuli for two incomparable responses in a situation where, if presented alone, each would yield a response." The various types of conflicts involve variations on this basic operation. The conclusions Lundin draws from experimental studies of conflict situations do not take us much beyond James' insights: the behavior of individuals in conflict is "impoverished" and "distorted." The type of conflict experienced determines the extent of vacillation. Anxiety accompanies reactions to conflict where aversive consequences are likely. Lundin's other comments on conflict and its management are merely behavioristic translations of the basic Freudian defense mechanisms. In the translation process, intrapsychic processes are interpreted as stimulus-response contingencies and are related to conditioning histories. In more human terms, choices would be explained by a behaviorist as having something to do with current circumstances and with past experience. This seems to fulfil two of our criteria for an adequate perspective on decision making. Yet when we turn to the modern offshoots of experimental psychology, in either cognitive-behavioral or cognitive-social psychology (both of which deal explicitly with decisions), the promise of enlightenment has not been fulfilled; the long relegation of subjective processes to a secondary, even epiphenomenal, status took a heavy toll.

Cognitive models

In the place of introspective accounts of actual decisions, models of "rational" cognitive processes were proposed and held up against inferior human judgment. From classical decision theory to its information-processing descendants, this practice has gone unquestioned. A logical model of what a typical decision involves is constructed; then it is demonstrated that we are incapable of adhering to such a model; and finally, techniques are devised to help us approximate it.

Classical decision theory, a field developed primarily by mathematicians like Pascal who were hired by gamblers to determine what constituted a fair bet (Horan, 1979), comes to these conclusions:

> A decision maker is by definition someone who is faced with the task of choosing between several alternatives. Each alternative will result in the realization of various objective and subjective values.

> . . . the bulk of decision theory concerns decisions made at risk. Risky decisions are those in which the values realized by the selection of a particular alternative are not certain. . . . Maximization of *expected* utility is the primary rule in risky decisions.

> Thus, when confronted with a seemingly uncertain decision, the (subjectively expected utility maximization) model would suggest culling our pertinent experiences, affixing probability estimates according to our best "guesstimates," and then adopting the maximization of expected utility rule.

> . . . personal decision making is best facilitated by utilities quantified by simple self-report scales.   (Horan, 1979, pp. 55–60).

A crude translation: decisions are difficult to the extent that we are uncertain about outcomes associated with the various alternatives. The best alternative to choose is the one most likely to have positive consequences in ways that the individual deems most important. To reduce complexity, it would be helpful to rank or rate our priorities and allow the arithmetic to indicate the appropriate alternative. As an illustration (I hope not a serious one), Horan tells us of Fred, who is trying to decide which of two room-mates to ask for a date. Fred assigns utilities to Gail and Debbie, an 8 and a 7, respectively. Then he estimates probabilities of acceptance of his offer: .4 and .5. "Expected utilities are calculated by multiplying the utilities by the subjective probabilities. Gail's expected utility is .32; Debbie's is .35" (Horan, 1979, p. 56).

The inadequacy of this approach, which has unfortunately become the model underlying a major theory of human motivation called expectancy-value theory, may not be readily apparent. The fallacy lies in the fact that for any given individual, an analysis of probabilities is largely irrelevant. If the young Arthur or Sir Edmund Hillary had based their decisions on the probabilities of succeeding at pulling the sword from the stone or climbing Everest, respectively, neither would have achieved a thing. Similarly, in deciding whether to try to become a concert pianist or a common music teacher, the equation in the former case (low probability, high utility) might lead one to choose the latter (high probability, moderate utility). The *meaning* of choices seems to have dropped entirely from consideration in this approach, not to mention variations in human capacities, motives, and other factors which render a major life decision *unique*.

The classical approach to decision theory can be termed *rationalistic* because it emphasizes the importance of logical cognitive operations in coming to ideal decisions. The reliance on quantification is supposedly justified by its greater trustworthiness. Subjective components are given their due in the subject's perceptions of value, but it is clear that values are more appropriately subjected to processes of *clarification* and *understanding*, than to quantification.

The rationalistic trend is definitely present in all current models of decision making in "mainstream" American psychology. For example, a four-stage model presented by Horan in *Counseling for Effective Decision Making* (1979, p. 175) synthesizes a number of models in the terminology of "cognitive-behaviorism." The predominance of a mechanistic logic is obvious here, a logic which serves to strip the decider from any contexts which contribute meaning to the decision being made.

In stage one, the individual conceptualizes the decision, constructing "a cognitive model of the troubling portions of the environment." Then, the individual surveys alternatives, seeking to enlarge the "response repertoire." Stage three involves the "identification of stimuli discriminative of positive or aversive consequences for each response" as well as other information gathering. Finally, "response selection," made possible by ranking potential responses and "implementing" the most promising one.

The abstraction in cognitive-behavioral formulations is intentional.

Sometimes it is justified by the argument that worrying about life-historical, social, or subjective aspects of a decision is impractical. Consider this passage from *Towards a Self-Managed Life Style* by Williams and Long:

> Our self-management approach obviously does not emphasize existential insights, attitudinal changes, or global inner processes to resolve human problems. We are denying neither the reality nor the periodic usefulness of such inner phenomena. Our contention is that a more manageable approach to solving your problems is to change circumstances in your personal environment. Without those environmental changes your problems are likely to continue.
> (Williams and Long, 1979, p. 19)

One cannot dispute the claim that environmental changes can alleviate life problems. Yet, as the interview with Mary indicated, environmental changes often have little impact on characterological dispositions and do not necessarily facilitate the real transcendence of life issues through insight, character development, and *subsequent* situational transformation.

We have skimmed important trends in American approaches to decision making in order to devote space to a detailed critique of a premier contribution to the subfield, Janis and Mann's *Decision Making: A Psychological Analysis of Conflict, Choice, and Commitment* (1977). This is a multifaceted work which presents several models of decision making, a detailed summary of important research findings, and a catalog of interventions for "improving the quality of decision making." The authors address the problems of "important life decisions" as well as policy making and group decisions. They are interested in the phenomena of indecision, procrastination, impulsive deciding, evasion of personal responsibility, commitment, and other significant experiences. Getting even closer to the core of our project, they attempt to answer this question: "Under what conditions will a person's feelings of self-confidence and self-satisfaction about a past decision be replaced by a dejected mood of post-decisional regret?" (p. 8). In other words, how should one go about making important decisions? What are the characteristics of a decision that is retrospectively viewed as a good one?

Janis and Mann present their model of ideal decision making with this preface:

> From the extensive literature on effective decision making . . . , we have extracted seven major criteria that can be used to determine whether decision making procedures are of high quality. Although

systematic data are not yet available, it seems plausible to assume that decisions satisfying these seven "ideal" procedural criteria have a better chance than others of attaining the decision maker's objectives and of being adhered to in the long run.

(Janis and Mann, 1977, p. 11)

The criteria offered are reproduced below. I urge the reader to imagine handling a personal decision in the suggested manner in order to get a real feel for this approach.

The decision maker, to the best of his ability and within his information processing capabilities

1 thoroughly canvasses a wide range of alternative courses of action;
2 surveys the full range of objectives to be fulfilled and the values implicated by the choice;
3 carefully weighs what he knows about the costs and risks of negative consequences, as well as the positive consequences, that could flow from each alternative;
4 intensively searches for new information relevant to further evaluation of the alternatives;
5 correctly assimilates and takes account of any new information or expert judgment to which he is exposed, even when the information or judgment does not support the course of action he initially prefers;
6 reexamines the positive and negative consequences of all known alternatives, including those originally regarded as unacceptable, before making a final choice;
7 makes detailed provisions for implementing or executing the chosen course of action, with special attention to contingency plans that might be required if various known risks were to materialize. (p. 11).

These points take into account one fact ignored by the previously discussed models – that people in the midst of making an important decision are under stress. They get anxious, frustrated, embarrassed, excited, or worried. The criteria specified above are designed to compensate for errors in judgment that arise because of "unpleasant emotional states" accompanying life dilemmas. Normal "information processing" is thrown off course by guilt, shame, or anxiety. This ideal model is called a conflict-theory model of decision making because it takes into account emotionality, a fact shoved aside by phenomenological and previous social psychological approaches to the topic.

The ideal decision outlined above should be kept in mind as we turn to the full conflict-theory model of decision making, which, the authors write, "applies only to decisions that have real consequences for the decision maker and thereby generate some discernible manifestations of psychological stress" (p. 69). Five assumptions about the "functional relationships between psychological stress and decisional conflict" inform the structure of the model. These assumptions (pp. 50–2) first link stress to the anticipation of loss or failure to achieve important goals and to the degree of commitment to a present course of action that may have to be abandoned. Given a high level of risk, "defensive avoidance of threat cues" occurs primarily because hope of finding better alternatives is lost. In other words, the decider who is under great stress because no solution seems ideal will not pay attention to the negative features of the alternative which seems most preferable. This "defensive avoidance" includes the "lack of vigilant search, selective inattention, selective forgetting, distortion of the meaning of warning messages, and construction of wishful rationalizations that minimize negative consequences" (p. 50).

Panic or "hypervigilance" results when time is short and signs of danger or loss are salient:

> Expecting that he will be helpless to avoid being victimized unless he acts quickly, the person in a state of hypervigilance fails to recognize all the alternatives open to him and fails to use whatever remaining time is available to evaluate adequately those alternatives of which he is aware. He is likely to search frantically for a solution, persevere in his thinking about a limited number of alternatives, and then latch onto a hastily contrived solution that seems to promise immediate relief, often at the cost of considerable postdecisional regret. (p. 51)

According to the theory, ideal decision making requires a "moderate" amount of stress. One should not care too much or too little about the outcome of the decision. "[E]xtremely low stress and extremely high stress are likely to give rise to defective information processing, whereas intermediate levels of stress are more likely to be associated with vigilant information processing" (p. 52).

Janis and Mann present a simplified flowchart of their conflict model (see *Figure 1*). The left column contains antecedent factors which initiate or impinge on the decision process. These are predominantly interpreted as "communication variables," "information," or personal dispositions, although "many other situational factors also function as antecedent conditions" (p. 71). The authors explain that:

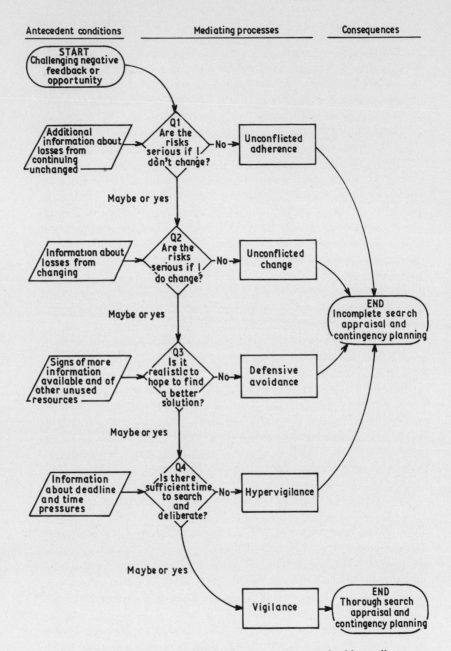

Figure 1 A conflict-theory model of decision making applicable to all conse-
quential decisions.
Source I. L. Janis and L. Mann (1977) *Decision Making*. New York: Free Press.

Communication variables are given prominence (rather than other situational or predispositional determinants) because much of our analysis of decision making focuses directly on the influence of warnings, reassurances, and other relevant information presented to the decision maker by the mass media, private counselors, representatives of reference groups, and other communicators.   (p. 71)

The middle column pairs questions posed to the self with models of coping with decisional stress. For example, after one considers the question, "Are the risks serious if I don't change?" one might move toward the coping style of "unconflicted adherence" to prior commitments, or move on to consider risks associated with changing.

It will be helpful to walk through the flowchart of Janis and Mann's conflict model, using our knowledge of Mary's situation (in Chapter 2) to concretize the steps.

The "challenging negative feedback or opportunity" which sets off the entire decision making process is the physical and psychic pain she suffers at the hand of her second husband. Moving directly to Question 1, "Are the risks serious if I don't change?", she will probably answer yes. If she is not convinced of this at first, she will gradually become sensitive to "additional information about losses from continuing unchanged." For example, she hears that her children might be taken away or she might come to severe bodily harm. Question 2 has her asking, "Are the risks serious if I do change?" Here, she imagines that her husband might retaliate if she left him or perhaps that she would be stigmatized for failing twice at marriage. To this point, we can see why Mary is stuck for the moment. Serious risks await her no matter which way she turns.

Moving to the phase of deciding represented by Question 3 ("Is it realistic to hope to find a better solution?"), Mary considers the lawsuit against the company that fired her in hopes that a reduction in financial worries will calm her husband, or failing that, to have the means to go through with a divorce. To the extent that she has lost hope, she will avoid considering possibilities which could actually resolve her dilemma (e.g. moving home again, seeking counseling, looking for another job).

A sense of impending crisis prevents Mary from feeling like she can wait around forever. She wishes she could defer action until her children are older, but fears that they will be hurt or taken away. This situation is likely to set up "hypervigilance," a state which is accompanied by anxiety and vacillation.

In Mary's difficult situation, the conflict model draws our attention to important factors contributing to her troubles, to the moments of questioning she is likely to pass through frequently as she tries to come to a decision, and to coping patterns which are bound to make her decisions less than ideal. Particularly descriptive are the states of defensive avoidance and hypervigilance. In the former, "the person spends little time thinking about the implications of unwelcome information" (p. 74). In the latter, the person "becomes obsessed with nightmarish fantasies about all sorts of horrible things that might happen to him, and fails to notice evidence indicating the improbability of their actual occurrence" (p. 74).

Defensive avoidance occurs in at least three forms, according to Janis and Mann. The first two, procrastinating and shifting responsibility for the decision to others, are common maneuvers. The third strategy, called "bolstering," exaggerates the positive consequences of the least objectionable alternative and minimizes its drawbacks.

At this point, we find ourselves wanting an explanation of these strategies. What is happening as one bolsters or procrastinates? Can these moves be understood, or must we stop with the simple explanation that these are failures of information processing?

The beginnings of the desired explanation are offered in Janis and Mann's analysis of preconscious biases and unconscious conflict in defensive avoidance. This account follows a standard, but opaque, presentation of the Freudian outlook on decision making, yet it is unique among mainstream approaches in suggesting a point-by-point correspondence between failures in information processing due to defensive avoidance on the one hand, and unconscious conflict on the other. The authors of *Decision Making* manage to work their way through the maze of experimental findings to the basic understandings advanced in these passages:

> On the basis of early emotional conditioning, social modeling, and direct experiences of extreme frustration and gratification, every person acquires certain emotional biases that are not wholly mediated or controlled by verbal thought sequences and language. Such unconceptualized biases may sway a decision maker to make apparently impulsive and irrational choices.

> As a consequence of disturbing socialization experiences and traumatic events in childhood, everyone is left with defensive reactions that prevent full awareness of forbidden sexual and aggressive drives. Defensive mechanisms prevent the coming into consciousness of certain wishes or goals and also prevent the full use of thought sequences in mediating the choice of the most appropriate action to be taken.   (Janis and Mann, 1977, pp. 95, 98)

Apart from showing how a Freudian analysis accounts for some types of defensive avoidance of information, the problem of understanding the roles of the life history, social processes, and life-structural constraints is too quickly abandoned here. Pointing to the effect of unconscious determinants on the course of consciousness does not enlighten us about the means by which those effects are achieved. The objectives of Janis and Mann's approach evidently fall into the first category of scientific interests discussed by Habermas as aiming for "technical control." They are not looking for ways of enlightening us about the meaning of decisions, but rather seek to emancipate individuals "from above" through systematized interventions which encourage a more faithful approximation to logical-rationalistic models of efficient choice. The life-historical and social contexts of a person's career choice, for example, are basically irrelevant to this model, except as these factors enter consciously into a decisional balance sheet or other fixed procedures for efficient decision making. Our interest is apparently of a different sort. We are seeking a reflective understanding of decisions. For this understanding, we turn to the phenomenological tradition, in hopes that its systematic description of consciousness will provide insights which take us beyond the rationalistic American approaches.

A PHENOMENOLOGY
OF DECIDING

Phenomenology is the philosophical movement and technique which claims as its task the descriptive study of consciousness. The most comprehensive analysis of the deciding consciousness is provided by Paul Ricoeur, a French philosopher, whose *Freedom and Nature* (1950) conforms to the rigorous specifications for phenomenology laid down by the founder of the method, Edmund Husserl (1859–1938).

Phenomenological investigations seek a "retrogression to the life-world" and a "destruction of the idealizations which veil the life-world" (Husserl, 1948, p. 41). If phenomenology fulfils its task adequately, it should lead us to glimpse the experiential structure of deciding in a manner not afforded by other approaches.

A few conclusions drawn from Husserl's study of "judgment" – which, of course, includes decisions – provide the foundations for Ricoeur's analysis.

In his *Experience and Judgment* (1948), Husserl shows that all types of judgment are made on the basis of assumptions about the world which are built up in the course of experience. We comprehend situations according to a "garb of ideas thrown over the world." These ideas have a certain rigidity and habituality which contribute to our ability to be decisive. They lend "assurance in decision and action in situations of life" (1948, p. 52).

The aim of this cognitive activity is to grasp how and what things are. In the general case of judgment, the goal is knowledge. In decision, it is knowledge of what to do that is sought.

The problem for the deciding consciousness is that many possibilities are present. Consciousness must manage to find a possibility which can be actualized *and* which matches the structures embedded in one's assumptions about the self in relation to the world.

For example, if I were trying to decide what to do with my life in terms of a career, it would not be enough to know that being an accountant is a possibility. That possibility would have to be capable of synthesis with previously held assumptions about myself and my role in the world. In psychological jargon, the possibilities I choose to actualize must co-ordinate well with my identity in order for a decision to be possible.

Husserl is aware that this is an incredibly complex task. From his observations, we may extrapolate a number of problems that might commonly arise as the deciding consciousness seeks a resolution.

In some cases, arriving at a decision will require a change of personal identity. This happens when no possibilities match one's sense of self. If a decision is required, the sense of self has to be adapted to actual possibilities.

Similarly, one may become lost in the complex consideration of various possibilities to the point of forgetting that these must eventually be related to one's personal identity. The frequent twentieth-century complaint about not being "true to oneself" or of feeling "alienated" and "estranged" may result from decisions of this sort.

In the practical decisions of everyday life, a pure and complete identity of self with a projected possibility is, of course, never achieved. Typically, one must say implicitly or subvocally, "and so forth," "and so on," in the midst of deliberation. Every possibility cannot be totally examined in the imagination, nor practically tested. This hints at a horizon beyond which deciding could always proceed but is rarely able to explore. Decisions are thus always made in the presence of a quantum of doubt. The decision itself may be fabricated primarily to cover over its shaky foundations and to escape the anxiety of doubting.

The construction of such pre-emptory judgments relies heavily on plugs which Husserl calls "empty judements." These are unquestioned assumptions which reinforce the logic of a decision. Examples: "I'm a Catholic, so I shouldn't decide to have an abortion"; "Let's get married now and worry about finances later." In any example, a significant basis for the decision would be left unspecified, unclarified.

For Husserl (1948, p. 309), deciding is a fluid process of questioning and answering. He concludes by offering hope that a sustained doubtful and critical attitude, that of *science* in the broadest sense, can rescue us from the quagmire of confusion. Deciding is "better" when it proceeds like the lawyer who, knowing that an adequate case has been established, continues to ask questions anyway – to suspend decision in order that it be "based on reasons, capable of nullifying the opposing possibilities completely" (p. 311).

An existential phenomenology

Ricoeur's phenomenology of deciding, which is presented in *Freedom and Nature* (1950), is an attempt to critique central concepts related to these complex moments of life: choice, hesitation, project, possibility, and so on. He takes up four different standpoints in the course of this critique, each one aiming at the heart of decision from a unique angle. First, he describes the relationship between the deciding consciousness and its future projects. Then, he analyzes the manner in which projects are connected to the self. Third, the role of desire and motivation in decision are clarified. Finally, he breaks the process of deciding into its temporal components: hesitation, attention, and choice.

Ricoeur's phenomenological account is quite abstract, yet it affords an essential framework for grasping the nature of deciding in general. A more specific psychology will only be possible on such a foundation. Inasmuch as Ricoeur's account is exceedingly complex (and obsessively faithful to the private jargon of phenomenology), I have reconstructed only the major points of his analysis here.

Ricoeur first distinguishes between a wish and a decision. The latter is accompanied by a sense of power or capability which could bring about the state of affairs projected by the decider. A decision thus signifies, designates, intends, projects "a future action which depends on me and is in my power" (Ricoeur, 1950, p. 43). Subsequent analysis pivots around portions of this statement. We look first at what it means to "project" an action.

> If we call "project" in the strict sense the object of a decision – the willed, that which I decide – we can say that to decide is to turn myself toward the project, to forget myself in the project, to be outside myself in the project, without taking time to observe myself willing. (p. 43)

The decisional judgment points "outward" but implicitly reflects the self which is doing the deciding. This parallels the general existentialist formulation that consciousness is a *consciousness of.* . . . This pointing or designating which occurs in deciding only points or designates in general (*à vide*) the structure of the event or action anticipated. Ricoeur holds that the designation of that which is to be done can occur with or without an image of that action. In fact, he implies that imagining may prove to prevent the occurrence of the action: "satisfaction with the image can charm me to such an extent that the imaginary becomes an alibi for the project and absolves me from the charge of carrying it out" (p. 45). Imagination can interfere with the realization of a project because it fictionally quasi-actualizes the intention, partially relieving the need for its accomplishment in action.

A decision is a practical judgment, not a theoretical one. It designates categorically ("so be it!") something to be done by me. Whereas a "wish" implies an alienation between me and the course of events, and a "command," even to oneself, is experienced as an alien force; decisions are commands and wishes only by analogy. There is an alienation in decision, but not between me and my body, or between me and the course of events; it lies in the duality of consciousness, between the *I* and the *me*, between the self as subject and the self as object.

One may notice that a future is implied in decision; a future is anticipated. Indeed, "to decide is to anticipate" (p. 48). This is a very complex anticipation, however:

> I leap from project to project across dead time, return to earlier moments, sketch the most interesting lines of future action, compress empty spaces, posit ends prior to the means which precede them, insert secondary projects into primary projects by gradual emendation or interpolation, and so on.   (p. 49)

Anticipation sets various "means in motion" as if a person were simply playing a role upon being given a cue. It creates a space for something to be done, setting aside a chunk of time in order that something be performed. This shaping aspect of decision is of extraordinary importance. Consider the little girl who "decides" at 6 that she wants to marry someone like daddy. The anticipation itself creates a structure which may never be called into question because that space has been set aside in time. We begin to see that decisions perform the function of giving form to a shapeless future, helping us to avoid the "trauma of eventlessness" (Seidenberg, 1972). So, when reality finally matches the anticipated moment, when the fellow with daddyish features turns up in the life space, the decision is already heavily constrained.

We cannot stress too much the extent to which consciousness is disarmed and powerless before its own drift into the future. It would be a great mistake to assume that only the past lies outside my control. The future is what I can neither hurry nor retard; it conditions the impatience of desire, the anxiety of fear, the wait of expectation, and finally subordinates the accomplishment of the project to the mercy of events. The past seems more basically beyond my control because it excludes the possibility that I might change it – it makes possible retrospection, but not action. But that there is a future which makes expectation and action possible is no less beyond my control. (p. 52)

What exactly is a "possibility"?

My power to do a projected action is clearly dependent upon a structure of events upon which I apply my action. Possibilities are thus structured by prohibitions, opportunities, obstacles, walls, routes, ways, resistances. "A possibility is what the order of things *permits*" (p. 53). *As a decision is being made one has no direct knowledge of the actuality that will be encountered when the action is to be performed.* A possibility is constituted by consciousness as it draws on memory, or on immediate perception. A possibility is, in short, something that we can analyze, call into question, or subject to an "archaeology" – a study of its historical emergence. Counter to our sense that possibilities exist "out there," they reside as much in oneself as in the world and therefore implicate the agency of the subject who is to do the action in relation to those possibilities. "For in doing something, I *make myself be*" (p. 55). This awareness leads Ricoeur to consider the being who is intending, the subject who decides. Three comments are made on the manner in which the self is implicated by a decision, when one says, "It is *I* who will do. . . ."

1 The awareness of self-implication in a choice is not always explicit, yet there is generally a manner of "looking at oneself" in the process of deciding which testifies to this self-reference. For example, I imagine myself at the desk with computer sheets all over it as I try to decide whether or not to be an accountant.

2 Self-awareness in the process of deciding, the "awareness of being the author of one's acts" is sustained, even predicated on, through one's existence in a social world: "Who did that?" "*I* did." The cumulative effect of such experience is to introduce subtly the Other into all deciding. "They" will not take responsibility, so I learn that *I* acted. This interpersonal structure is transformed into its future modality as projects are planned.

3 Since the self is not implied unless a project is considered, self-reference is assumed prereflectively. This is in fact an origin of the term *project*: the self is projected into the action to be done,

and in the tentative decision, a commitment or binding of self to project is accomplished. Only then can the self be reflected on as an object of consciousness, because until that moment there is no object toward which consciousness can take up an external standpoint.

The issue here is self-reflection in deciding and projecting. How is this possible and how might we make better sense of it?

When I am thinking about something that I am to do, I construct a representation of myself. This leads some thinkers to assume that somehow the reflecting consciousness turns back on itself, goes outside of itself in a sense, then returns in a suspension of the usual external orientation of consciousness. These gymnastics are unnecessary, Ricoeur argues, if we keep in mind that an awareness of a "practical reference to myself" motivated deliberation in the first place: I have some need to satisfy or some problem to solve or task to accomplish. In other words, a certain self-consciousness is the foundation of the judging consciousness. Only secondarily, when we reflect on the reflecting, do we explicitly realize that "It is *I* who will do . . ."

This comes as no surprise to anyone who has noticed that our common expressions about decisions indicate self-reflexivity: I make up *my* mind; in French, "Je *me* decide," or in German, "Ich entscheide *mich*." Ricoeur sees this structure of consciousness as the basis of both freedom and alienation. Alienation devolves from halting at either the subject or the object pole; freedom is maintained through a willingness or ability to attend to one pole then the other, in "an interior dialectic by which I alternately accentuate myself and the project, exalting one by the other" (p. 61).

Ricoeur has yet to clarify the nature of human motivation. He is well aware of the tendency to confuse natural causes with human motives. The latter do not conform to the cause-effect relations of the physical world, because motives have no meaning apart from the project which bases itself on them. "The motive cannot serve as the basis for a decision unless a will bases itself on it" (p. 67).

Metaphorically speaking, a motive is the base from which I thrust myself forward in decision. And when we seek to ground our motives on some foundation, we are seeking *values*, "reasons for our reasons." For Ricoeur, this relation of decision to motive and motive to value is crucial to action: "I do my acts to the extent to which I *accept* reasons for them" (p. 78). "The highest form of will is the will which has *its reasons*, that is, one which bears at the same time the mark of my initiative and the mark of its ancestry" (p. 66).

So, to decide means first of all to project a practical possibility of an action which depends on me, second to impute myself as the author responsible for the project, and finally to motivate my project by reasons which "historialize" values capable of justifying them (p. 84).

Deciding in time

To this point, Ricoeur has held the "birth of choice," the moment of decision, in suspension. This was necessary in order to view the structure of deciding in a broad existential framework. By abstracting the decision process from temporality, it remained a structure with a future-orientation, involving an issue *to be decided*. When the historical-temporal setting of deciding is restored, we quickly see that certain modes of consciousness that are central to the process have been ignored, for example, hesitation, search, attention, and the *fiat* (the leap or command of choice):

> the deciding will cannot be reduced to a terminal act, to a final *fiat* bursting suddenly into the warp and woof of an internal situation which makes no allowances for it. . . . Even if [the choice] erupts as a sudden change in indecision, its leap takes place within a willing consciousness and its surge does not mean that prior to it the will was absent or null. . . . The *fiat*, though it represents a discontinuity, springs from within a certain continuity of voluntary existence.
> (Ricoeur, 1950, p. 137)

Given the temporal dimensions of choice, our task is to understand decision as having a history which "appears as the awakening, birth, and maturing of a meaning" (p. 135).

Hesitation, by definition, precedes the moment of decision. It is usually seen as a way of avoiding choice or as a period in which a choice is being sought. Ricoeur, following Husserl, emphasizes that it is as much a matter of a disunited state of consciousness: "I am not *one* in indecision." Accompanying this disunity is an anxiety about the lack of a choice, a desire to fill an absence.

In hesitation, various strategies are checked out. One can justify indecision by declaring impotence: "I am not up to it." Or it can magnify its sense of power and opportunity: "Just think, I could do any of these things." Perhaps a real empowerment is sought in hesitation; it is a search for a strategy which will work. Implicit is a certain doubt about the self. The disunited self, the self which senses conflicting motives is not *sure*: "I hesitate precisely because the world is an ironic question: and you, what will you do? Each tentative project is like a stammering response whose progress is delineated by an outline of closed and open roads, of obstacles and implements, of openings and blank walls" (p. 139).

This sense of being under the gun is complicated by the fact that the world moves along as one hesitates. Others move, others choose, society changes. Often the need for hesitation disappears as one's question is answered by the experience of someone else: "Ah, so it is possible to survive a divorce" (a friend just did so); or, "No, it isn't wise to try to jump the Berlin wall" (someone just got shot doing so); or, "Yes, the money you earn being a doctor is worth the ordeal of med school" (after visiting a doctor's home, pool, and condo).

Even though self-doubt may be relieved by developments of the social world and the movements of others, hesitation may also stem from the feeling that one's intentions or even the decision itself, are not one's own. In the mode of consciousness which might be called imaginative role-playing, different selves are tried on, much as some individuals try on and reject several evening outfits before settling on one to wear to a party. This is clearly a case of confused intentions as one approaches an ambiguous setting. And to draw on the dressing-for-a-party analogy further, one is often inclined to sidestep the responsibility for a decision altogether by trusting the opinion of another. Similarly, one suspects that hesitation may arise from a sense that the decision being made is actually someone else's (often the case among siblings or across generations), or when someone has dumped his or her decision on to another who is willing to take responsibility for it.

What does this lead to? First, we see that indecision is the expression of a confused web of intentions. The vagueness of certain emotional experiences may be responsible here, since "affectivity is essentially disordered" (p. 144), one can endlessly attempt to specify emotional impressions. In some "regions" of the affective world, the self is unable to locate itself, to find firm footing.

Second, we must be aware of the possibility that the practical situation has the power to make a decision for one, by overt deadlines, by traditional patterns, by force.

Third, hesitation is a period of improvisation. It may be the locus of creative deciding, or of endless testing of unfeasible possibilities. Consciousness is capable of all sorts of fancy syntheses which are pleasing yet not at all practical.

Finally, Ricoeur emphasizes the role of values in shaping the hesitating consciousness in relation to a social topography which may include the ethics of all the ages of civilization as represented locally by

family, class, profession, nationality. The person situated in society is
not merely a collection of vague affects, but is actually attempting to
resolve his own distortion at the intersection of specific "duties"
through his decisions. In fact, the person emerges as a *person* only as
indecision is resolved in some way by taking stances, positions – by
making decisions.

Ending deliberation

Ricoeur concludes with two related issues: the means by which the
internal debate of deciding is ended and the relation of the moment of
choice to its history.

What is it that a choice brings to an end? How is it possible to stop
deciding, to make a decision? To answer these questions we need to see
that attention is the means by which deciding proceeds and halts. "The
power of stopping the debate is no other than the power of conducting
it. . . . Choice in a sense is a fixing of attention" (p. 149).

It is easier to describe what attention makes possible than to say how
it works. Attention can be guided, or allowed to drift. It can be careful
or loose. It is clearly a matter of character, interest, understanding, and
so forth, yet it is, in essence, the power of making objects appear.
Attention itself can change the way objects appear and is at the source
of originality of vision through the power of *bricolage* (patching things
together somewhat haphazardly, but with a purpose always close at
hand). Attention thus helps us to "clarify" projects and motives.

"Deciding" is not a unitary sweep of consciousness, but rather a
broken series of fragments of attention interspersed by practical
concerns, other decisions-in-the-making, and sleep. We cannot
assume that the latter are unrelated to the decision at hand, or that
decision making does not continue at some level when conscious
attention is not being paid to it. Many so-called intuitions or insights
emerge as resolutions to decision problems in the midst of attention to
supposedly unrelated matters.

Now, what happens with attention when a choice is made? Can we
say that it is fixed on a specific project? This would be an accurate
assumption if the project were already clarified at the point of decision.
Typically, it is not. What has been decided upon is the general "shape"
of the project. Its "interior" has yet to be explored or elaborated.
Hence, choice is a fixing of attention within a specific framework to
which one is committed, however temporarily. Choice resolves the
previous deliberation and "genuinely inaugurates the project."
Alternatives may remain to be decided between, but these exist within

the boundaries of a larger project which has been univocally accepted by the subject. The occasional difficulty of deciding may reside in the requirement that at least some framework be accepted as a foundation. Since this amounts to a simplification of the self and its possibilities, there is often a sense of sacrifice or loss which accompanies choice, however great the exhilaration of forward movement.

Given this phenomenological description of deciding, two "readings" of the choice point are possible (see Ricoeur, 1950, pp. 168–81). On the one hand, it can be seen as a break, a cutting off, or, on the other hand, as a continuity, something which follows from its historical development. Many theories of choice fall into one camp or the other, failing to resolve this paradox.

The first perspective sees choice as an original and novel act, based on a thrust or a leap. Only in the choice itself do motives for it take on a definite form. Choice is seen as a pulling up of oneself by the bootstraps, a command to oneself.

> Because man finds himself in a corporeal, historical situation, because he stands neither at the beginning nor at the end but always in the middle . . . , he must decide in the course of a brief life, on the basis of limited information and in urgent situations which will not wait. Choice surges forward in a context of radical hesitation which is a sign of finitude and infirmity, a sign of the constriction of human existence. I am not divine understanding: my understanding is limited and finite. (pp. 174–5)

This perspective carries us toward a position where the subject is seen as choosing constantly. Every action could be called into question. Every choice is seen as a creation of values.

The second reading of choice, highlighting continuity, runs as follows: in seeking a choice, one tests multiple projects and seeks to clarify reasons for doing them. The project "ripens with its reasons" until the choice naturally recognizes their validity or compellingness. In a sense, one comes to an agreement with oneself in choice. Choice might thus be seen as the last in a series of judgments which have a logical course. This last judgment would be a resolution of prior judgments, the best practical summary of what is to be done. The choice is thus only a keystone, a natural conclusion.

Limitations of phenomenology

If we were to sit down, in a sense, with Ricoeur's ideas in mind, to face a decision problem, how would we see it? What manner of reflection does his point of view encourage?

First, it would be clear that my decision has to do both with something I am to do, a project I will commit myself to carry out and with the sort of person that I am and will be. Automatically, it becomes a question about whether or not I am to continue to engage the world according to intentions embedded in previous projects or to break with them to form projects which embody new understandings of myself and the world. The fact that I am in the midst of deciding implies that some aspect of myself is at issue. I must decide whether to extend specific meaningful relations, involvements, or ways of living into my future, or to upset them. The decision thus involves a subjective relation to my history, to the person I have been. Similarly, it allows me to reorganize my subjective grasp of affective intentions. As Ricoeur states, my emotional life is essentially disordered. I could ceaselessly reinterpret my emotional reactions to possibilities and current projects in the light of prior experience. That process would shift my view of how I want to engage the practical world and might alter the values and reasons for my actions.

Ricoeur's outlook leads one to ask a number of questions which seem to stop short of a level which could be characterized as critical self-reflection. I would ask, for example, what do I want to do? What am I seeking to accomplish? Even, what values am I choosing to realize or to make a part of history? But would I be inclined to ask – if I adopt the standpoint of existential phenomenology – why do I want to accomplish this project? How does it come to have any meaning to me? Why actualize these particular values, rather than others?

Ricoeur's standpoint helps us to accomplish an initial penetration of the naive stance toward deciding. It undermines a tendency to see one's projects as dictated, or to carry them out without reflection on their purposes. Yet, it seems to me that this movement in itself is insufficient.

This claim can be justified in the light of Mary's dilemma (Chapter 2). Mary's decision to sue the company that fired her is a commitment to a project. It has a definite relation to her experience with that company and the damage it has done to her situation. She could ask, "What am I trying to do?" and answer herself, "I am getting revenge against the big guys who take advantage of the little guys," or "I am trying to attain financial security." "What does it mean about me that I am doing this?" "That I stand up for myself as I have never done before." "What values am I trying to actualize?" "What reasons do I base my decision upon?" "The right of an individual to fair treatment; society's obligation to provide for the needy; the principle of justice for all." Whether or not this imaginative construction of Mary's outlook is accurate is not at issue. The problem is the extent to which a phenomenological perspective leads us to and elucidates the possibility of self-deception.

For all the insights provided by Ricoeur's account, it apparently *leads one to cut short the process of reflection at a point where either "common sense" or rationalization dominate*. It assumes the transparency of the subject to himself rather than emphasizing the gaps or fault lines in subjectivity.

The single interview I had with Mary does not provide sufficient evidence to establish firmly the following interpretations, but it is possible to indicate here a manner of reflection which subverts the mode of rationalization permitted by a phenomenological self-understanding. Each of these possibilities indicates a realm of meaning, or a context of intentions, which for one reason or another is not immediately accessible to the self-reflecting consciousness:

Could Mary's desire to retaliate against the company be primarily an indirect expression of anger at her husband for the treatment she receives at his hands? If so, wouldn't her aims be better served by attention to that sphere of her life? This is a form of reflection on what has been called the "life-structural" context of a decision.

Is Mary setting herself up for another beating, this time at the hands of men who are even more powerful (unions, lawyers)? Is her fascination with men who have money leading her into another situation which looks promising but may actually impoverish her further? If so, are there ways in which she could change her life or herself which would help her achieve autonomy from this characteristic tendency? These questions stem from a view of the "life-historical" context of decisions.

Could Mary see her dilemma as yet one more example of what capitalist patriarchy imposes on women, as any socialist-feminist analysis would conclude? Could this understanding allow her to redefine her goals in opposition to her husband's desire to keep her in her "proper place" and motivate her to participate consciously in one of the revolutionary movements of her era? If so, what constraints would she have to grapple with? What social resources might she draw on?

In fairness to Ricoeur, we admit that he acknowledges this latter "social" context of deciding, but offers no insight into the manner in which decisions are mediated by objective sociohistorical forces. Following Ricoeur, if one is not aware of these factors by reason of education or cultural training – and typically these important trends are systematically masked by the distortions of ideology – it would be impossible to construct a life in relation to the realities of one's own time.

PSYCHOANALYSIS VERSUS DECISION

We have seen that decisions are means for resolving conflict over possible courses of action. Conflict is experienced inwardly as a jumble of emotions, as a heightened sensitivity. Since this intrapsychic conflict is the keystone of psychoanalytic theory and the main target of psychoanalytic practice, it is striking that analytic scholars have been relatively silent on the psychology of decision making. Psychoanalysts are ideally positioned to witness the dilemmas and decisions of their patients, but they have chosen to focus their writing on the former, on the ambivalence which makes deciding difficult, rather than on the processes which make deciding possible.

Strangely enough, despite all the insight to be gained through the technique he developed, Freud himself was, at least at one point, content to surrender his own major decisions in life to forces of the unconscious. He told his friend Theodor Reik:

> When making a decision of minor importance, I have always found it advantageous to consider all the pros and cons. In vital matters, however, such as the choice of a mate or profession, the decision should come from the unconscious, from somewhere within ourselves. In the important decisions of our personal life, we should be governed, I think, by the deep inner needs of our nature.
>
> (Clark, 1980, pp. 50–1)

This attitude on the part of the founder of psychoanalysis may have played a role in excluding the topic of decision making from the arena of classical Freudian topics. In the realm of clinical technique, however, Freud seems to contradict his advice here, as we see in a moment. Indeed, it is frequently said that psychoanalysis has as its basic goal the capacity for decision.

Over seventy years after the birth of psychoanalysis, Rangell, a noted scholar of psychoanalytic ego psychology, was able to write:

> I wish to present and highlight one idea, namely to add and make explicit "a decision making function of the ego" among the inventory of ego functions. . . . To extract this function and treat it on its own, and to establish its centrality in psychic life, is not only for the purpose of adding what I consider a vital link in our theoretical framework, to explain more fully the sequence of psychic events, but also because it is a nodal point of enormous external and "applied" importance. With the latter I am referring to a contribution which I believe psychoanalysis can and should make to understanding the decision-making process of man. . . .
>
> As a token of the high order of priority which this subject occupies on today's human agenda, a large literature has recently developed on the subject of human decision-making. While this includes a cooperative effort by a wide spectrum of disciplines, psychoanalysis remains conspicuous in its absence.   (Rangell, 1969, p. 599)

In the text that follows this passage, the author continues to express surprise that the role of the ego as a mediator of intrapsychic conflict of the sort which accompanies any important decision making has been ignored. This is an issue of extreme importance, adds Rangell, citing the common psychoanalytic knowledge that *unconscious determinants of action are particularly powerful in conflict situations of the sort that beg for decision.*

It is in trying to comprehend the relative silence of psychoanalytic theory regarding decision making that we begin to appreciate its contribution to our project.

Keeping in mind the basic Freudian hypothesis that all mental life is overdetermined, that its meaning derives from its relation to the entire history of the subject, we can scan the psychoanalytic vocabulary for instances of the terms "choice" or "decision." The latter is rarely used. "Choice" is found in two peculiar settings, both of which are saturated with a sense of inescapable overdetermination. The term "object-choice" is used to designate the determined attraction of one person to another on the basis of unconsciously sensed similarities between one's experience of the latter and some important past figure. The determinants of object-choice are complex and perhaps infinitely specifiable.

We also find the term used in the phrase "choice of neurosis," referring to the problem of understanding why a person chooses a particular defensive resolution of infantile conflicts. Again, it is hardly a choice in the sense of the term which comes down to us from the philosophers of free will and personal responsibility. As far as psychoanalysis is concerned, choice is a term reserved for phenomena that are determined in a very complex fashion (Freud, 1913).

The explicit use of the term "choice" in this ironical manner expresses the foundational assumption that no human act can be properly described as a true choice. Instead, all is *character*. Where the term choice implies at least a partial freedom (in general usage), character is associated with fixity and the determination of subjectivity by automatism. All deciding should thus be seen as mediated by the embeddedness of conscious processes in the structure of character. There is continuous debate regarding the meaning of character and even about its usefulness as a category in the human sciences, but we can define it generally as a structure of intentions which a subject seeks to accomplish in social life which bears the imprint of experience in relations with important others over the life course. As we saw in Chapter 1, character refers to the manner in which an individual's ongoing involvements in the life structure are constrained by interaction paradigms established in previous life phases and which now dominate the repertoire of images of self-in-relation-to-others and form the core of self-understandings.

To understand the particular relevance of psychoanalytic theory to decision making, we should now examine the technique as it encounters decisions in clinical practice. The following passage condenses the basic insight to be had in this regard. It is taken from Freud's "Remembering, repeating, and working-through" (1914).

> One best protects the patient from injuries brought about through carrying out one of his impulses by making him promise not to take any important decision affecting his life during the time of treatment – for instance, not to choose any profession or definitive love-object – but to postpone all such plans until after his recovery.

In the course of treatment, the analysand seeks to gratify lifelong yearnings in his or her relationship with the analyst. The analyst interprets these rather than satisfying them or playing out the drama the neurotic is attempting to repeat. Freud's advice to analysts signals the possibility that the analysand will try to "discharge" tension heightened in the "transference" of wishes on to the analyst by seeking substitute gratification outside the analytic situation. This "acting out" supposedly reduces the possibility of recovering the latent wish or of achieving insight into the object-relational paradigm which compels the analysand to act. Freud's concern was not only to avoid delaying the cure. He realized that neurotic choices generally express sado-masochistic impulses and exclude action in one's best interest.

Freud's advice has been tempered by subsequent generations of analysts as the increasing length of treatment made it impractical to postpone all major life decisions. In place of making patients "promise" not to make decisions, analysts now urge them to understand as fully as possible any projected actions which might alter life significantly (Van der Sterren, 1966). In the face of threats of potentially self-destructive acting out, analysts are to interpret vigorously the meaning of the action in relation to the transference and encourage the patient to wait until the impulse is understood (Abt and Weissman, 1976).

Psychoanalytic skepticism is justified by the repeated encounters analysts have with patients who come in saying they want the exact opposite of what their actions indicate. Lacan, the radical French analyst, describes a typical situation poetically:

> what motivated the patient in his search for health, for balance, is precisely his unconscious aim, in its most immediate implications. What shelter, for example, does recourse to analysis have to offer him, in order to re-establish peace in his home, when some hitch has occurred in his sexual function, or some extra-marital desire! From the outset, the patient admits to a desire, in the form of a temporary suspension of his presence at home, the opposite of what he came to propose as the first aim of his analysis – not the restoration of his marriage, but a break with it.   (Lacan, 1973, p. 138)

We thus need to consider the analyst's attitude toward the content of a decision and to the manner in which it is framed. Generally, it will be likened to the manifest content of a dream or other multisided phenomena (slips of the tongue, obsessional ideas, etc.). It cannot be understood until associated ideas, desires, fears, and images are explored. The report of the decision conflict is scrutinized for traces of the underlying conflict of which the decision problem is merely a symptom. Ferenzci writes:

> It is well . . . not to accept too easily the patient's stressing of the urgency for an immediate decision, but to consider also the possibility that such apparently very real questions have perhaps been

pushed into the foreground unconsciously by the patient, whereby he is either clothing the analytic material in the garb of a problem, or his resistance has taken this means of interrupting the progress of the analysis. . . . Of course a patient may really on occasion have to decide an important matter without delay during treatment; but it is well if on these occasions, too, the doctor plays as little as possible the part of a spiritual guide, after the fashion of a *directeur de conscience*, contenting himself with that of analytic *confesseur* who illuminates every motive, those, too, of which the patient is unconscious, as clearly as may be from every side, but who gives no direction about decisions and actions.   (Ferenzci, 1919, pp. 94–5)

Ideally, though, Ferenzci states beforehand, "The doctor's endeavor must always be to postpone decisions till the patient is enabled, by a growing self-reliance due to the treatment, to deal with matters himself" (p. 95).

The psychoanalytic warning, then, is that coming to a decision cuts short the process of understanding the roots of a dilemma. In order to understand a decision problem, one must look at its manifest features as epiphenomenal, as symptoms of deeper issues. Difficult decisions sit astride meaning-complexes which could be subjected to lengthy artic- ulation. Indecision thus stems partly from the fact that dilemmas are *signs* (Lorenzer, 1976); they represent more than they pretend to and are detached from their actual objects. To try to decide one way or the other about the manifest issue may seem pointless because of these hidden intentions. Ideally, major decisions would be made only after major lacunae in self-understanding have been eliminated. In particu- lar, the axes along which one's intentions contradict each other could be brought to light and the dichotomy confronted. This process entails an analysis of character. The structure of decision dilemmas, in fact, reveals character. Issues preventing choice, or forcing impulsive choice, metaphorically express conflicts which are experienced in many spheres of life and repeatedly over the life course. Often a decision will even be framed in a manner which permits the active repetition of strategies which have failed previously, because to overcome the underlying conflict would be, in some sense, more painful.

The psychoanalytic account of intrapsychic conflict is central to our subsequent interpretation of life narratives. In the following sum- mary, which ties together concepts developed to this point, it becomes evident how decisions may further self-deceptive practices. Some authors hold that psychoanalytic theory offers an account of "self- deception" – a term arising in philosophical debates in various technical senses. The term indicates any self-misunderstanding which is primarily due to the general non-transcendable characteristics of the human condition, e.g., finitude, separation in space, emotional life, etc.

Fingarette (1974) accounts for self-misunderstanding along lines suggested by Freud's late paper on the "Splitting of the Ego in the Process of Defence" (1940). Acknowledging that self-deception is not adequately accounted for by stating that an individual holds false beliefs, Fingarette defines self-deception as an issue of *disavowing* aspects of one's engagement in the world. Self-deception thus implicates a subject's "identity." A particular identity is established as the subject is reflected in his or her own consciousness. That image may bear a more or less authentic relation to the individual's history and intentions. As we have seen, the constitution of character in the process of socialization is founded partly upon the repression of certain unacceptable desires. In so-called "regressive" actions, these achieve partial expression. To avow the intentions which motivate such relatively automatic action would threaten the synthesis, so precariously achieved, which makes up the subject's identity.

Fingarette demonstrates that when an intention is hidden from the conscious part of the ego in this manner, it is not being hidden from the id, the superego, nor the ego. Each of these agencies has a hand in either the maintenance of the impulse or its management and would thus be "aware" of it. What then is the point of defending against acknowledgement of the impulse? Paraphrasing and translating Fingarette into terminology we have employed, a possible answer runs as follows. The projects in which a subject is engaged or anticipates accomplishing are founded on assessments of reality. Reality, however, is not something directly apprehended. The reality of the subject is being construed as a "representational world" (Kernberg, 1977) constituted, as Husserl indicated, over a series of interactions with the world, for the most part, other people. In everyday experience, we forget that the portions of reality to which we attend in our various projects sustain our interest because we have *needs* that we seek to satisfy. In early experience, certain attempts to satisfy those needs were met by punishment, pain, disapproval, loss or stress, with the consequence that conscious hopes of gratifying them were abandoned and reality itself is no longer represented as capable of providing for them. The identity of the subject forms partly in order to define the self as not having those needs.

The intriguing hypothesis one can draw from this outlook is that the self-deceptive aspect of any major decision derives from the defensive tendency to focus on appealing aspects of the project to be carried out in order to disavow unacceptable wishes which are either frustrated in current engagements or to be secretly satisfied by the accomplishment of the decision and the action it sets up. The urge to make a decision may derive more from defensive requirements – the attempt to maintain a coherent identity or to shore up defenses which are weakening due to stress in a particular sphere of life, for example – than from practical necessity.

Standing back from the main trends of psychoanalytic theory discussed to this point, it is clear that much is left out: the tangled relations of the Oedipus complex, the dynamics of transference phenomena, the processes of sublimation, identification, and character development. What has been sketched here is a core of theory relevant to all types of decisions. When we take even this minor portion of the Freudian corpus, it is clear that the recurring foundational ideas involve histories of interpersonal/intrapsychic relations. Each relationship is a context in which meanings arise and can either be grasped, ignored, or suppressed. Lacan says, for example, that the unconscious is the censored chapter of my history. A context in which I have lived is not acknowledged. I live as if it were not there, as if it had not happened. But this intentional forgetting makes that chapter even more powerful in determining what will follow; "the thing which is meant to be warded off invariably finds its way into the very means which is being used for warding it off" (Freud, "Notes upon a Case of Obsessional Neurosis," 1909b).

As nearly all of the commentaries and observations advanced in the remaining chapters are heavily influenced by psychoanalytic principles, we will not pause to introduce these essential ideas at this point. It is sufficient to note that, although decisions *per se* do not loom large in the vocabulary of psychoanalysis, it is the psychoanalytic perspective which most radically calls the certainty of choice into question and provides key parts of the framework for a viable psychology of decision making.

LIFE STRUCTURES

Interlude

Merely psychological approaches to deciding reify the process. They abstract the dilemma from the contexts which breathe life into it and commit unpardonable conceptual ploys, for example, dehistoricizing the decision, reducing it to the simple representation of an infantile wish, restricting the intent of a decision to its practical referents, or ignoring the sociocultural contribution to our styles of deliberation.

These problematic tendencies in the psychology of decision making are troubling not so much because our theories will be inaccurate, but because institutional interventions based on such misunderstandings have a serious impact on the quality of individual lives and social life in general. I have in mind computerized self-assessment or vocational choice programs, interest inventories, routinized counseling or psychotherapeutic techniques, and quantitatively determined personnel selection, to name a few of the more prominent choice-molding practices. Many experts view these developing patterns of institutional practice as benign, but given their capacity to shore up rationalizations and extend the domination of relatively exploitative groups, it is hard to convince oneself that these tendencies will not lead to greater alienation and estrangement.

Why do so many knowledgeable people condone these problematic approaches to decision making? If we back up far enough, there seems to be a generalization to problems of decision making from the nature of our usual orientation to *tasks*. This leads to a linear schematization of psychological processes. Consider, for example, the step-by-step procedure we must follow to put something together, or to fix something, or to accomplish a goal. In conceptualizing the process of deciding, this linearization merits a serious challenge. The troublesome schema appears in various guises:

need – planning – decision – action
problem – clarification – solution – achievement
impulse – imagination – compromise – satisfaction
desire – fantasy – choice – assertion

In each case, mentation is precipitated by something external to it. A strategy for coping with that impinging event is sought and settled on in a decision. Then, action or some consequence is effected.

The psychology of decision making, perhaps because it takes the term psychology in too limited a fashion, cuts off aspects of the deciding process which make it human. The contexts of meaning we delineated earlier must be considered at each point in this schema, and seen as the foundation and end of the entire process: What is the social context of a particular decision problem? What life-historical factors affect this person's decision-making strategies? How do life-structural features impinge on the capacity to reflect, to make a commitment, and carry out effective living? What social response will a decision receive? How does a choice relate to previous choices? What unanticipated life-structural consequences will follow from a choice? How does one person's decision become a problem for another? What constraints and advantages do certain languages and cultures bring about in the way individuals decide on life issues? What institutional features lead to poor decisions?

Psychological theory is essential to answer these questions, but it is not sufficient. For example, if we address the perpetual issue of freedom versus determinism, little can be said on the basis of the general schema above. It would appear that one is both constrained by problems, but free in coping with them. Most analyses locate freedom in the deliberation phase. These conclusions take us nowhere. If we instead hold that individuals are free to the extent that they interpret problems, deliberate, commit, and act with a deep awareness of the contexts which mediate and determine their own perspectives and inclinations, then a useful statement is being made. In short, decisions try to lift themselves up as brief moments of pure consciousness, denying their embeddedness in life, in a particular life. Psychology has been blind to this fact.

This chapter develops the notion of the "life structure" as a first corrective to psychology's blindness. Chapter 7 investigates implications of the life-structural perspective for our understanding of transitions. Then Chapters 8 and 9 interweave these new understandings with a life-historical point of view on the development of character and the problem of repetition in decision making. Finally, in Chapter 10, the broader social implications of this interpretive perspective are noted.

The emergence of the adult life structure

A life structure can be analyzed in terms of the projects of which it is composed. Projects can be categorized according to their degree of "totalization" (to borrow a term from Sartre, 1960):

projects in process (a book being written, a chair being made, managing an account, raising a child, developing a friendship)

group projects (bowling team, political action, religious services)

unrealized or abandoned projects (the unfinished painting, the skill never used, the long-neglected friendship)

totalized projects (accomplished goals, satisfied dreams, the trip around the world, the Nobel Prize won, the construction completed)

uninitiated projects (imagined possibilities, things one always wanted to do but hasn't tried).

A relatively constant process of decision making determines the order and progress of each of these projects. Involvement in each entails specific psychological modes, energies, and moods. The various projects intertwine in a person's self-understanding and form the basis for our sense of well-being, progress, usefulness, and meaning.

Any project which is regularly a part of the life structure will be referred to here as a "life sphere." This is a temporally-bound system of action, affect, and awareness. A life sphere is what one hears about in response to questions like, "What do you do?" or "What are you up to these days?" Life spheres are also the typical "units" of major life decisions. A life structure does not change all at once. Life-structural transformation is more a matter of negotiating the internal aspects of life spheres and their interdependence.

Engagement in a life sphere is a complex activity. The psychic moments entailed include attention to images of self-in-action, to the reactions of others, to the effects of one's activity, to the fantasied goal of the activity, to emotions aroused, and so forth. In each sphere, a person will have specifiable intentions and unrecognized motives, all of which seek satisfaction over the course of engagement in the life sphere.

What does the concept of the life structure contribute? Its first function is to serve as a corrective to the subjectivism that psychological studies naturally adopt. Any particular psyche with which we are fascinated is an aspect of a specific person who lives in a particular place and time, who has a body and does something each day. These basics must never be pushed out of the picture.

Second, the concept might serve to encourage a reflective stance – a break with the natural attitude which does not require self-questioning. Anyone who paused to consider seriously how his or her life structure might be objectively described would have cause for concern. Productive life changes are frequently instigated by what we might call a life-structural mode of reflection. This would lead, for example, to an inquiry into the meaning of one's work over a decade, the impact of one's hobbies on efforts at parenting, the state of one's health in relation to various habits, and so forth. The concept of the life-structure suggests that each of us is "in the driver's seat" and therefore to some extent responsible for the activities in which we find ourselves engaged. When our attention is focused on *self-initiated changes* in the structure of everyday life, then the relevance of the life-structural point of view becomes even more obvious.

To varying degrees, life structures are set up by major life decisions. Levinson (1978) acknowledges this but does not emphasize decision making in *The Seasons of a Man's Life*. Early in the book, however, he wonders, "How shall we go about describing and analyzing the life structure? The most useful starting point I believe, is to consider the *choices* a person makes and how he deals with their consequences" (p. 43). The implications of this assumption are traced in this important passage:

> We have to consider the meaning and functions of each choice within the individual life structure. As a component of the life structure, every choice is saturated by both self and world. To choose something means to have a *relationship* with it. The relationship becomes a vehicle for living out certain aspects of the self and for engaging in certain modes of participation in the world.
>
> The primary components of the life structure are choices, in the sense I have just described. The components are not features of the self, such as motives or abilities, nor are they features of the world,

such as institutions, groups and objects. In characterizing each choice, however, it is necessary to understand the nature of man's relationship with it, to place it within the life structure, and to see how it is connected to both self and world. (Levinson, 1978, pp. 43–4)

Following Levinson's suggestion, we will examine the emergence of the adult life structure of a man in his late twenties, called "Bill." Particular attention will be paid to the choices he made which played an obvious role in setting up the current structure of his everyday life. We will also try to clarify the "meaning and functions" of some of the life spheres set up by those choices.

When I first interviewed Bill, his life structure could be characterized roughly as follows:

He lives in a small three-bedroom home in a middle-class suburb of Cleveland with his wife and three children, aged 8, 6, and 2. He drives forty minutes to work each weekday in downtown Cleveland where he works in the headquarters of a computer firm as a systems demonstrator. Bill knows none of his co-workers on a personal basis, but interacts with several of them daily. His performance is satisfactory, but not energetic. He is happy to return to his home when his work schedule permits. In the evenings, he plays with his children frequently, watches TV, converses with his wife about the day's doings. Once a week, he spends the evening playing basketball with a group of men his age. On weekends, Bill watches sports on TV and plays with his children and the neighbors' kids, and goes to church with his family. This routine is broken every two or three months by visits to his family in Indiana on holidays or birthdays. Bill's mood as he moves through these spheres is generally placid, earnest, and mildly positive; yet he describes a puzzling frustration as he drives to work, exaggerated excitement over a great play on TV sports, and bothersome temper outbursts directed at his wife or children.

If we are to develop a sense of the decisions which led Bill to this relatively conventional life structure, we need to position it in his life history. This imaginative historical reconstruction will help us to bring into relief contradictions which simultaneously block the life structure in its current state *and* provide momentum for modifications. We should look carefully for clues as to the meaning of Bill's angry outbursts, for they seem to belie the tranquility of this middle-class existence.

The dawn of the 1950s finds a factory worker, his wife, and daughter settled in a small Catholic farming community in Indiana. They are expecting an addition to the family. It turns out to be a big healthy boy.

Young Billy thrives in the rural town. He will remember numerous childhood days spent at his paternal grandfather's farm – cutting grass, eating apples, running in the yard of the farmhouse, coming in to a big farm lunch. He also plays at the other grandfather's gas station. There he develops mechanical skills, fiddling around with car parts under the old man's watchful eye. When Billy is 6 his father quits his factory job to take over that gas station.

As Bill grows up he notices that his father is gone much of the time:

> He worked a lot and when he wasn't working he played baseball a lot. There was one big game when the scouts from the pros were there to see pitchers. My dad hit a home run. It ended up 1–0 after seventeen innings. That was a great day. It felt good seeing the scouts talk to my dad.

It's okay that dad's away as long as he's the hero, but there is also the problem that when dad *is* at home the scene is rather stormy:

> It wasn't a good marriage but they stuck it out. Maybe it would have been better if they hadn't. Dad used to bowl and play ball, go drinking and come home drunk. My mother probably had a reason to be mad for that, but she was also very anti my father's family. I don't know why. I never asked. I guess you block it out or try to block it out. I kinda was against my mom because she was against Dad's family so much. That bothered me more than Dad drinking. But I just grew up, blocking it out. Life went on. . . .

Sometime in early elementary school Bill meets the girl he will eventually marry, but he does not take to her at that time. There is something about playing with girls that makes him uneasy, anxious. Bill will recall very few specific incidents from childhood, but one vivid memory involving girls will stand out:

> I was 7 or 8 years old. Three neighbor boys were out back. We had gone across the street and there were two or three girls over there. They were in this garage and I cut my hand on the glass over there reaching toward them through a window. I told my mom that it wasn't over there that I got cut. I said they were over here with the glass. They were chasing us with the glass or something. I don't know why I didn't tell her the way it happened. I don't know if I wasn't supposed to go over there at this girl's house, or what. I didn't want to get into trouble for some reason whatever it was. I was afraid of trouble.

What was it like getting into trouble?

A oneway argument. You were wrong. Yell. Yell. Yell. [Laughs]
She'd yell at you, say you were bad, send you to your room and she'd
be mad for a while. Doesn't sound so bad, now does it? As to why I
didn't tell her the truth, I don't know, but there's something else
there I'm sure.

In this memory, an important organizing theme of Bill's emotional
life is crystallized: the free play of life is dangerous, spontaneous action
and natural desires will be punished, better to go along with what
authorities say, safer to be involved in activities where it is clear what is
right or wrong.

As Bill enters junior high school, he starts to work at his father's gas
station on weekends and in the evening. His extracurricular activities
are limited to sports but he starts to be at home as rarely as his father.
At work there is little intimacy between father and son. Conversation
is limited to the topic of sports and automobiles. Bill feels part of a
family mainly on the Sunday afternoon outings when the family goes
to watch the father play baseball. Bill also begins to excel in sports.

What time remains in Bill's busy schedule is filled with "farm club"
projects, church activities, and a paper route. For many years, Bill
attended 6 am mass with his father before delivering Sunday papers to
the sleeping community.

The little girl from second grade, Susan, reappears on the scene in
high school. Bill beings to date her in his sophomore year. He is quickly
becoming a local sports hero and she is a cheerleader. She intuits that
she will one day marry Bill and tells him that, but scares him in late
high school by dating a fellow from a rival town who has a "nice new
car with a four-speed stickshift." Bill gets mad and stops asking her
out, sensing that the family station wagon is not up to snuff. Bill turns
away from females altogether and runs with the boys instead.

The impression that adolescence passed without any hitches cannot
be sustained in light of what Bill remembers of his home life in those
years. Recalling confrontations with his parents, Bill describes a typical
evening situation:

You want to do something, go out or whatever, and they say yay or
nay and you were stuck with that. You went into the other room and
got *mad*, very hot-headed. If you got angry back, you'd get hit. Very
crude . . . I don't know, maybe it worked; maybe that's the way to
do it. I don't see that it's the right way myself. Maybe that's a
differing I have with my parents.

Over ten years later, Bill is still giving his parents the benefit of the doubt. He has a hard time trusting his own sense that there was probably a better way to raise children, perhaps because he struggles with the same tendency to be hot-headed. We look into this further in a moment.

Finally, the little boy who didn't want to go to school at first finds himself nervously giving the valedictory address at graduation from high school. It is striking that all of these childhood experiences will blur to the point that when I asked him to recount the story of his life in our first interview he tried to dismiss it all. All of the hurts and little joys, the excitements and let-downs fade into this sweeping cover story: "I grew up in a small town in Indiana. A little town of about 500 people, and everything was hunky-dory there. Everything went along fine, and then I went to college."

Now a pause to develop a broader perspective on Bill's youth. In the late 1960s a small Catholic farming community offers up its pride and joy to the outside world. He is big and strong. He is as smart as they can make him in their rural school. He has a solid faith in God which he will not abandon and he knows the importance of family life, both from the good times and the bad. He has been literally whipped into shape and has come to see the world in terms of a few rigid categories: good-bad, rich-poor, male-female, right-wrong, country-city, work-play, and so on. He is proud of his grand country and is open to taking what it offers him. His plans, hardly reflected on, are to go to college and get a job. Looking back, he describes his state of mind at the time in this way:

> I didn't have any real visions of what I was going to do, okay? I've never had a good clear picture of what I wanted to do in life, okay? Be that bad or good. . . . Some people get the idea that this is what they're gonna be, they get a good idea of what they want to do and follow a plan. And then there's me: I get out of high school and I want to go to college, but I have no idea of what I want to take up . . . I was valedictorian of the class in high school, so I should have known what I wanted to do, or at least thought I should. So I went to college. I went to Notre Dame. And I liked math a lot, so I got involved with computers and it was kind of neat, but, you know [implies not *that* exciting] [Laughs].

How can we make sense of this account? What is its "logic"? We would be on fairly safe ground to assume that Bill's relatively strict upbringing inclined him not to trust his imagination. His impulses and fantasies only get him in trouble, as in the scene where he got his hand cut chasing the girls. He follows the path projected for him by his subculture by going to Notre Dame and plays the safest career game by moving toward a job in computer science.

At college, Bill studies hard, plays intramural sports, parties occasionally, and continues to go to church, usually by himself. He goes home as often as he can to date Susan and to work in the gas station. (Notre Dame was then an "all-boy college.") Susan visits Bill for the big homecoming football game and the two begin to talk about *when* they will get married. The question of *whether* to marry is hardly debated. During Bill's junior year, they plan a summer wedding. He explains his attraction to Susan in these words:

> She was good-looking, I guess. She was a good person, a hard worker. There were nine kids in her family and she was the oldest of the girls. She would run the household while her parents were in Florida. She was a good person . . . honest, took care of kids; she told you what she was thinking, didn't lie. . . . I just knew that by being married we'd be together all the time. That's what we wanted. That's what I wanted.

Bill and Susan get married as planned. The central sphere of Bill's adult life structure thus falls neatly into place. One gets the impression from the passage we have considered, and others not presented here, that Bill has gone along with Susan's idea of getting married both because she will be a good mother to her future children (and to him) in contrast to his own mother, who also contributed to the decision by teaching Bill never to question a woman's authority.

Bill soon graduates with a degree in computer science. Graduation day is an event he will remember fondly; it is one of the few times in his life when his family comes *to him* in his honor.

Education for Bill has been vocational training, pure and simple. He would have certain advantages in the world of work, but it is not much help to Bill when he graduates, at least not in terms of opening up career opportunities. His country is at war in Vietnam and his post-college decisions are more than slightly constrained by that fact, in league with his unquestioned patriotism:

> When I got out of college, I was going to get drafted [low lottery number], and a month before I got out, I said, "Hey, I'm gonna get drafted." So I went down and checked out the Air Force, Army, and Navy to see . . . because I was also gonna have a kid in a couple of months and I didn't want to go to Vietnam. The options in the Air Force looked best, plus Susan's brother was in the Air Force, and he

said, "Oh yeah. You got a college degree – go and be an officer; it will take you three months, a little bit of grief. . . ." I looked into it and that's what we decided to do. The only thing we planned on then was that we were going to be in the Air Force for six years and that was that.

So another important decision was made, not hastily, but in a highly determined situation, and with unanticipated long-term consequences.

Bill is soon a captain in the Air Force and serves as a navigator on flights to Europe and South America. He loves flying and marvels at the places he visits, but it really bothers him to be away from Susan and their first daughter, often for weeks at a time.

Apart from the excitement of flying and traveling, Bill does not enjoy the Air Force. He resents the hierarchical organization and status games. He even dares to violate social taboos by playing basketball with the enlisted men. Bill's primary satisfactions continue to come from family and sports activities.

Susan bears two more children while Bill is in the Air Force. When their six years are up, they have saved enough to put a down payment on a house and Bill is anxious to leave the service to be with his family more consistently. He logically looks for a job in computers, but finds that he will have to take a big pay cut (some $7,000 less) because his college training is now obsolete and his Air Force skills are not transferable. He wants to go into programing and be involved in the technical aspects of computers, but being desperate to get out of the Air Force, he lets himself be talked into working as a computer salesman.

Bill is miserable as a salesman ("I'm not a big talker"). He requests a transfer to another department and is placed midway between sales and technical work; he demonstrates computer systems to potential customers brought in by the salesmen. This is where we find Bill at age 28. The job has its advantages, but he would prefer to stay home and also finds that his pay, $18,000, is insufficient to meet the needs of his family.

Bill's story leads us to an important insight about the development of adult life structures. The experiences which accumulate as one moves towards "independent" adult life bear down heavily on initial choices. These are rarely autonomous decisions. The very powerful forces of socialization enter into the categories applied to dilemmas and determine to a large extent which dilemmas are taken up for consideration. We thus find most young adults in this society making occupational and/or marital decisions as if there were no other dilemmas available. Subsequent decisions are thus primarily strategies for undoing, altering, or improving initial commitments to particular life spheres in young adulthood.

Bill's current life structure thus seems to have "fallen into place." Decisions did play a role in determining this outcome, but Bill leads us to believe that few of his decisions were difficult, that he actually had little choice along the way, and that this pre-emption of his choices hardly bothers him. Bill's passivity is to some extent conditioned by his attitude toward authority. He goes along in order to avoid trouble. This pattern leads to a disastrous stalemate in the development of his adult life – a stalemate which indicates why the organization of life spheres needs to be consciously composed and *willed*.

The interdependence of life spheres

The conscious choice of a life pattern hardly ensures satisfaction, but it is a step toward meaningful engagements in the world. Bill's abdication of choice in the sphere of work, for example, contributes to his present predicament. Work is primarily seen as something which prevents him from spending time at home with his children:

> I like the job because it gives me the freedom to be where I want to be. It's up to the individual to use his head and take time off during the week. But they like to keep track of where you are. And you wouldn't want them to find out you were just at home.
>
> At the office people don't work that hard. As long as the customers are happy. Keep the customers happy and get the product to them. The job takes someone who can work on their own. . . . I wouldn't like a guy standing over my head and saying you gotta do this and this. I like it loose, with nobody standing across the top of you.

Bill clearly finds it difficult to invest himself in his work. It hardly seems to mean anything to him: "If you're using your head, you'll take a lot of time off." I suppose that this is partly due to the nature of the work, but there is also the problem that his upbringing has not given him the option to believe that work could be an activity which related to a purpose beyond "earning a living."

At the time of our interviews, Bill was up for a yearly review at the office. I asked him what he would tell them.

> I wanna quit. Naw, not really. Do you want to know the truth? I'm not asking for something I'm not worth; I really need the money just to pay the bills for the house, food, and clothes. And I'd like to know if there are areas where I can advance quicker and what I can do to

increase my salary. I'm gonna tell them that I'm considering taking
on a second job. I wanna go back to the Air Force and fly.

Here, Bill is touching on a dilemma which tears him apart from the
inside out, and which may underlie the outbursts which puzzled us
earlier. His first impulse is to get out of the business, but he rationalizes
this feeling away. He cannot afford to be so irresponsible. He finds that
inflation is eating away at his income. He can no longer make his
payments without cutting out other essentials. If his boss can't come
up with more money, he will have to go into the Air Force Reserves –
an outcome he would not particularly regret. This decision would take
him away from his family for two weekends each month, but might
placate his daughters who nag him to take them out for hamburgers.
Susan tells him he should go back to the Air Force not for the money,
but because he likes to fly. He admits that he would like to try flying
again, but worries that the kids will bug him for not being at home. The
kids, on the other hand, tell him to go back into the Air Force fulltime.
As he portrays the situation, they don't value his presence that highly –
they want a higher standard of living. Even Bill admits that he would
like to get rid of the "old clunker" he drives. Bill is also embarrassed
that his kids wear hand-me-downs from neighborhood families. He
struggles to make himself feel better about the situation: "You don't
need money to have a good family life. It might be good for the kids to
have less treats."

Bill told me later about the outcome of his yearly review. Given his
apparently stressful financial situation, it must have been quite a blow
to hear that he would not get a significant raise. But Bill sides with his
employer's point of view, suppressing whatever anger he might have
felt. He seems to have become anxious about asking for things to which
he previously told me he had a right. Here's his account of how it went:

It went okay. I told them [two supervisors] I needed more money
like I said I was going to, and they said, "What can we do?" and
laughed. But they *have* given me raises, and I told them I knew they
had to work within guidelines, too. They just can't *give* everybody a
bunch of money. Then I told them I was going into the reserves.
They made some comments asking why and are you going to be
around when we need you and I said "Yeah, as far as I know." So
other than that, it was just talking back and forth. It's not a
hostile-type atmosphere, but they weren't able to say. . . .

How did you feel afterward?

Basically satisfied, but I wasn't sure I got my point across. I couldn't even keep it straight. If anything, I was bewildered about what I told them. I tried to explain that I needed more money and they said "Well, we see you want more money" and nothing else. They missed the complete story.

Bill then attributed his financial difficulties to the high cost of living in his particular suburb (which happens to be in the moderate range as Cleveland communities go). He also reaffirmed that he *had* received raises in the past and that according to company salary guidelines he was doing as well as he could hope.

We already know that he steps back from conflict or argument. We saw this in the confrontations he had with his mother, where he chose to go to his room rather than insist on his right to determine his own adolescent lifestyle. His father seems to have modeled this retreat for him. Bill's quick identification with the standpoint of his employers was a move which probably relieved him of anxiety about losing what little he does get from the people who provide for him.

Bill's need to maintain a positive attitude in order not to lose what he already has is shored up by a number of life mottoes which emphasize kindness and interpersonal respect. Much of our dialogue centered around this struggle to suppress a number of consequent self-images: that he is lazy, that he is not a good provider, that he is not the kind of person he feels he should be. The glaring contrast between his angry outbursts and his ideal self-image has him confused, but because the relations between the sphere of work and his homelife are not direct, he is unable to grasp the core of the problem. Hence he continues to believe in a world where kindness will earn its reward, where social inequalities are not so important in contrast to the gift of life itself, and where money is not important:

When you're playing sports, it's how you play the game, not if you win or lose, and life is the same way. It's not if you are making a bunch of money, or if you can do this or that; it's how you play the game, how you get along with the people, how you treat them.

For me, having a family is a big kick. Having kids makes life worthwhile. Watching them grow up, trying to teach them something. Hopefully you'll put something in their head so that when they grow up they'll do something, treat people right. Not necessarily be a great person and invent something and make a lot of money, but learn how to live, be kind, and courteous. . . . Kids can grow up and experience the world and see how great it really is. It might be all messed up economically, but there are physical features of the world that are beautiful. There is a world to *see* out there.

But money and unfairness keep intruding into the would-be paradise in a very irritating way:

> I'm basically a decent person, but there are always shortcomings, things you'd like to do different, a certain image you'd like to live up to. Like the way you treat your kids. You don't want to lose your cool and blow your top.

How would you like to be different?

> I wouldn't get depressed or down about money. I wouldn't worry about that so much. I would find more ways of getting up and helping someone. There are always times when it's easy to walk the other way and not get involved. I should be living more the way Jesus did. Trying to help people, being kind, passing those attitudes on to my kids. It's easier to train kids than to change adults.

What do you try to teach your children?

> I don't know, just basic values, I guess . . . what's right and wrong and that monetary things and some things along those lines are not that important. Money's there; you've gotta have money, I guess, to live. And you've got to meet certain basic needs of an individual, but beyond that point there are certain values that are more important than money. Like how you live your life, how you get along with people and how you treat them and that. *Maybe I'm lazy, but I don't think that happiness is a bunch of money.* I find happiness in my family and through the kids.

Even though Bill deems money to be relatively unimportant, he worries about the lack of value he places on his work. Perhaps he knows that if he could care more about it, his financial problems would be less pressing.

> Well, some people would say I'm not motivated enough at work, maybe, to really be a go-getter to where I'd spend 24 hours a day and live at work and try to get ahead there. Some people do that and when you talk to them, they have their point of view, too, that they want to get ahead so they can give their family everything, but to me that's giving them what isn't important. Spending some time with them, enjoying life, and trying to help them grow up and adjust to a world that is pretty complicated is more important.

The problem also arises in the context of talking about his marriage but is again minimized:

From the way I see it, our marriage is pretty good. We've grown a lot together. We've learned that there are a lot of things that are important that rank way ahead of making a lot of money. It's much more important that we're happy, healthy, and don't seem to have a whole lot of big problems. . . . We've learned to look at little problems that get you from day to day, we try to put them aside and try to realize that they're not that important. It's more important that you are together, that you can express feelings, enjoy life, and be happy and do things with your wife, and kids. I don't know what else I can tell you . . . I'm very happy.

But expressing feelings and enjoying life are on occasion antithetical in Bill's experience of marriage. His temper tantrums obviously trouble him:

The three or four little things that you don't bring up sit and grow in the back of your head. Then you hit a brick wall and say, ''We're gonna do it my way.''

What kinds of things lead to that?

Little ones. I wanna watch football. I wanna go play basketball. I wanna go see my parents.

These are not random examples. They clearly point to a desire to return to the golden days of boyhood – a time when he was a hero in sports, admired by his community. I failed to see this at the time and asked him if there were any bigger issues that contributed to marital arguments.

Don't know if we ever had one. Most problems are little ones, but they lead to big confrontations. You get stubborn and bull-headed about it. A week later you look at it and say ''Boy, was I dumb to let that bug me.'' I hold things in more than my wife. She has more of a temper, but I've learned that maybe it's good to blow it off and get it out of the system. It boils within you.

Why do these things get you angry?

I don't know. Something wrong with me, I guess. You get to thinking you want to do something and she'll want to do something else. You let it get under your skin and things tend to boil up. If you realize that a lot of stuff is trivial, you just flush it away and forget it. It's more important that you are together and can share time and experiences.

Bill invokes the rhetoric of caring and kindness every time he is about to judge his situation unfavorably: I don't have enough money to make ends meet, *but* that's not important. It's how we treat each other that counts. How does he manage this anger? The emphasis on kindness caps it off, but he has also told us something about how he experiences his anger as it comes into his awareness: a system boiling over, that needs to be flushed out. It is merely excess feeling, nothing which could have a meaning for him. Below we see the counterpart to this feeling; a specific psychological state which prevents a blow up. He described this feeling after I had asked him if there existed aspects of himself that he considered "wild and crazy" or impulsive in some way. He said that he could not think of any, but went on to account for the fact that he was not thinking well:

> I don't know. I'm just blank this week. The kids were sick one night and I wasn't feeling too good. Boy, I just feel funny today. Things just passing me by. I'm not all there or something. It's bad news. Once in a while I feel like I'm in a vacuum. My head's plugged up, just a void. Just letting the world pass me by today.

It is possible that this numbness is the consequences of massive defenses against rage. Evidence for this came near the end of our final interview, when I asked Bill again if there were important aspects of his life that we had not touched on. He thought I must be asking if there were not some secret desires to reveal. His example of things he would *not* do give us some indication of the discomforting aggressive and passionate fantasies which might steer him away from giving his daydreams too much free play:

> My life hasn't had any real big problems. I haven't been, what? . . . convicted of murder, or haven't gone through three or four wives, don't have a mistress, ha. I haven't hidden things. I'm sure it would be a lot harder [to participate in these interviews] if right away you got into something like if the guy had a mistress, or if I ripped off the gas station, robbed the place, or something. Maybe from talking to people you can tell if they're hiding something. Where the hell were we?

These are also far from being random examples. His father had a gas station. He needs money from a bank. He has been involved with only one woman in his life. Bill's frustration and confusion here was partly due to my assumption that he simply needed permission to talk about his "wild and crazy" fantasies, but it also stems from a negation of anxieties as each of these images is expressed and denied. (We know from Freud, 1925, that these denials testify to the existence of un-acknowledgeable wishes.) At the time of this inquiry, I hadn't realized that we had already spoken about Bill's most private realm of consciousness when we discussed religion and prayer. These experiences are indeed expressive and they help us to understand the structure of Bill's daily experience, especially the cycle of anger, suppression, and vacuity he has described. The religious realm of his life also serves to mediate the relations between the spheres of work and family, allowing problems to go unresolved. If we wonder why he is unable to break past the stalemate which interferes with life in both spheres, these understandings show how the pressure is kept from becoming too intense, keeping boilovers to a tolerable minimum.

Bill first states that he doesn't have the time for doctrinal debates in religion: "I don't go in for all this analysis like they do to the president's speeches. Religion is just basically being good. Each person has to decide for himself." I then asked him if a personal relationship with God played a part for him and if he had an image of God. He defines God, it turns out, using exactly the same terms of reference he applies to himself. God is perfect on each. Bill falls short.

> God? Just a big cloud. I have more an image of Jesus. What's in the book, page 22? . . . He's nothing I can picture. He's someone who would be the ultimate in good, would not fail in any tests, wouldn't blow his stack. But he's very human in that he's not worried about money or having a new car, he's concerned about people and giving to people of himself to make them happy. Since he feels this way, he created this universe and put us here and *has given us the ability to make a decision as to what we want to do*, if we want to help people or don't want to help people.

Why is it important for us to make this decision?

I think there is something after you die, somewhere that will show the good and the bad. It won't be a place to punish the bad or make the good feel they are superior. The bad will realize they were bad and feel sorry that they were bad. The good will enjoy happiness. In heaven people will feel good. Everyone will be happy. You won't have to worry about a new car, or food, or a house, or whatever.

What is your relationship to God like, then? Do you pray?

When I pray, I relate to Jesus. God sent us Jesus to show us the way. There's a closer bond to Jesus because he lived here. When I talk to God or Jesus, it's like talking to a psychiatrist, okay? My good psychiatrist who I can talk to and say, "Gee, this was great. Thanks for that. I really felt good about that." I don't know, I think personally that more people should pray like this, not tied up in saying a prayer out of a book, just trying to talk to Jesus, thank him for some stuff, ask him for stuff, just bounce things off, "Boy, this was rotten. Why did this happen?" Just clear your mind and let it ooze out. It helps to have someone to do that with. It clears your head and makes the next day start over fresh. That's the way Jesus and God operate. If you talk to them about it if you do something bad, you know you have done it. You can either do it again or not do it again. And the first step to not doing it again is to admit that you've done something wrong, and to say, "I did something wrong, now do I want to do it again? No, I don't want to." You have to express it to someone. And that way, the next time it comes up you're more likely to remember, "I don't want to do it." As opposed to doing it and saying "I screwed up" and going out and leveling ten people and then the next time it happens you do it again and you level ten more people [laughs]. So I look at him as a psychiatrist. It's a lot cheaper, too.

A crucial point regarding life structures may now be advanced. The spheres of a life structure, although temporally distinct, are nevertheless linked. Freudian theory has referred to this linkage as displacement, but that concept does not quite capture the sort of balancing of spheres through a mediating sphere that Bill accomplishes. We are generally aware that problems at work can spill over into our moods at home, but it is not generally acknowledged that entire life spheres may function primarily to defuse aggravations in other spheres. This would happen most often, I suppose, when one feels unable to alter or leave the disturbing sphere of life. For example, when young adults "wake up into" a job they don't particularly enjoy, as Bill did, they may be prevented from directly changing this central sphere by other commitments they have made: finances, contracts, even tradition. The attendant compensatory spheres (hobbies, "vices," and so forth) quickly become ruts and also a part of one's "identity," as activities one could not do without.

In Bill's case, the displacement is directed partly at his wife and children, but that is softened through his ability to go to the Good Father in heaven for forgiveness. This move dissipates his frustration over not being the good provider and hero to his children that he would like to be, but short-circuits the possibility of confronting directly the dissatisfactions in the sphere of work which are destabilizing his homelife. This interdependence of work and family spheres has changed its character recently due to changes in macrosocial structures, leading Bernard (1981), for example, to comment on the decline of the "good-provider" role. The traditional role adopted by Bill's wife probably aggravates the situation, because the relation of spheres is reciprocal. His wife's motherly style may sustain an infantilization which hinders his progress at work. At some level, Bill knows that life problems can have these characteristics:

> When I lose my temper, it bugs me, because it's *dumb* most of the time, and it cuts down on communication. It's the biggest problem with most problems . . . lack of communication. The problem is usually not the real problem, it's like a smokescreen. People don't want to talk about the real problem.

Bill eventually decided to join the Air Force Reserves – a move which by altering one aspect of his life structure, namely, the way he spends two weekends each month, resolves in a compromise fashion his conflicting expectations of himself. It allows him to do some work he finds more satisfying, but leaves his main worksphere intact. It will alleviate financial pressures, but will take him away from his family more often. In this decision, we get a glimpse of the powerful structuring effects of the social context of everyday life. In a literal sense, the social order wins out by encouraging him to its defense in order to meet needs attendant to the consumerist orientation of his children which was, in the first place, instilled by the economic order of the society he defends.

Ruts, routine, and regularity

> The mass of men lead lives of quiet desperation. . . . An unconscious despair is concealed even under what are called the games and amusements of mankind.
>
> When we consider what is the chief end of man, it appears as if men had deliberately chosen the common mode of living because they preferred it to any others, yet they honestly think there is no choice left.
>
> (Thoreau, *Walden*)

A rut is a "habitual pattern of response that is culturally learned and sanctioned, and which prevents us from acknowledging a wider range of possibilities in ourselves and in our relationships" (Gutknecht and Meints, 1982). In the rush of "moving on" or "keeping up," the implications of trivial events are not addressed. Minor choice points are passed up in automatic decisions based on the mechanical operation of values. Walls are built up. Accommodations are made. Compromises are silently negotiated.

Even while life steals one by one our reasons for living, our successive centers of gravity, it at the same time, often unnoticed by others, almost always unnoticed or at least unrealized by ourselves, replaces them with petty satisfactions that solidify a person and enable him to pass from yesterday to tomorrow – those hidden props to so many lives that seem to have nothing left in them.

(du Bos, 1962, pp. 39–40)

Each life structure comes to be sedimented by routine. Even attempts to escape from routine become ruts themselves. Are we doomed to live in ruts? Will everyday life always be organized in such a way that we have no trouble conceptualizing it as a *structure*?

This question can be transcended by analyzing the role of decisions in relation to life structures. It turns out that the problem lies not in routine itself, but in the nature of one's projects.

Since life structures are composed of ongoing projects, they are continually undergoing subtle transformation. Yet, there are periods in which little outward change can be observed, where a person's pattern of commitments and activities is relatively predictable and regular. One would think that major life decisions aim to change routine, but a life-structural analysis shows that the contrary may be equally the case – that decisions may function to allow a routine to continue or that routines may actually serve to fend off the need to come to a decision. What is the basis of the need for *routine*? The "modern consciousness" is not likely to look kindly on it, but seems to be tempted to seek its regularity. Consider the following passage from the autobiographical notes of Franz Kafka:

I am almost thirty-one years old. . . . The uniformity, regularity, comfort, and dependence of my way of life keep me unresistingly fixed wherever I happen to be. Moreover, I have a more than ordinary inclination toward a comfortable and dependent life, and so even strengthen everything that is pernicious to me. Finally, I am getting older; any change becomes more and more difficult.

(Kafka, 1914, p. 105)

Kafka's complaint is surprising, given the interesting use he made of his structured time. The existence of a routine clearly does not indicate a deficit of "openness to life." But life structures often come to be experienced as rigid or beyond one's control. Many adolescents conspire to avoid falling into ruts as adults. They cherish spontaneity and irresponsibility because they see too many adults who, having fallen into the jaws of routine, are unable to extricate themselves. How can it come to be so difficult to change aspects of life structures that are unpleasant, or even "pernicious," as Kafka complains?

Part of the answer lies in the fact that it is difficult to maintain an "engagement" with every life sphere. When we let go our concern in a sphere, the situation (usually others) gains the upper hand. We see an extreme case of this in Camus' *L'Etranger*. There we confront the tale of a man who happens to be completely detached from concerns about the direction of his involvement in the world. Asked if he would like to transfer from Algeria to a better career opportunity in Paris, he says he doesn't care. Asked by a lover if he wouldn't like to get married, he replies with the same "Cela m'est égal." It takes a certain energy to be engaged in living and takes even more to contemplate change and carry it through. Detachment is not a non-relationship but a defensive relationship, where feelings and concern are blocked off in order to avoid responsibility and disavow intentions.

Camus' character fights off the necessity to make decisions by detachment. He imagines himself to be free by not choosing and assumes that is what he wants to do. Conversely, it is possible that what one does as a matter of routine is hardly what one wants to do, but is instead a shield against productive changes in one's life.

The benefit of routine lies in its capacity to serve as a foundation from which to grapple with the most troublesome spheres of life. We all know people who seem unable to cope if they miss their regular round of golf, morning coffee, or meditation session. Routines also serve to prevent the unexpected from erupting into the tranquility of day-to-day living. In many cases, the routinized life structure has been achieved only tentatively, precariously, having been carved out of a life which was previously chaotic, unmanageable, and anxiety-ridden. For some of us, therefore, the establishment of a stable life structure is a major accomplishment. But the problem still remains that routine may be preventing progressive life changes, or even blocking their consideration.

Most of my interviewees had changes in mind which for one reason or another they were putting off. Major life decisions often have a very long gestation period. During this phase they are hardly formulated as decisions *per se*, but are merely mild concerns, anticipations, parts of uninitiated projects, or issues in which each of us is implicated by reason of shared culture (e.g., whether to marry some day, to commit oneself to a cause, to smoke or not, etc.).

A 30 year-old subject called "Ken" told me he anticipated having to decide whether to move or not within the coming two years. It turned out, after a series of interviews, that this masked a deeper concern about having children.

For five years, Ken and his wife had maintained a frantic routine which to some would hardly appear to be one. They played sports, traveled, partied, and, in the midst of all that, managed to build a very large house in preparation for family life. At the point of our interviews, the house was receiving its final touches. I was surprised to hear Ken talking of a move. It became clear that the frenzy of activity was a way of living it up before settling down to have children, or even of making children an impossibility. With work on the house no longer called for, the question of when to have children was beginning to be an issue. Ken admitted that he had no real desire to have them, but that his wife was eager to begin a family. So, by conceiving the need to move Ken was creating a new barrier in the forthcoming life structure which would serve the intentions underlying the current one. Both the routine which made "settling down" impossible and the projected decision to move, which would require building another house, served the purpose of screening off the more serious issue of whether or not to have a family.

So, even before a decision is officially claimed as a decision-in-the-making, its anticipation may establish defensive regularities in current spheres of life and lead to strategies to be decided in the near future about issues which will still prevent confrontation with more anxiety-arousing or conflict-ridden concerns.

The stable life structure, with its rush of events, and projects, and commitments, is rarely organized in a manner conducive to self-reflection or to the discovery of the most pertinent issues to be pondering. Seen in the broader context of one's personal history, life strivings, and social position, the organization of daily life loses its character of arbitrariness. The organization of a life structure may reveal a number of decisions which have been and are being made without conscious deliberation. This fact suggests that one could augment personal efficacy by reviewing frequently the relevance of current involvements to overarching life goals.

TRANSITIONS

Our existential analysis of deciding pointed to the embeddedness of this curious process in *time*. This experience we call time is not the abstract flow we imagine it to be. It is constituted by the events and activities of daily life. So to say that deciding is a temporal activity is to acknowledge its direct relation to practical involvements over a period of days, weeks, months. What follows is a collection of observations on the impact of everyday life on decision making in each of its phases. Although this is a continuation of the life-structural analysis developed earlier, we begin to see again the extent to which life-historical considerations enter into any full account of the meaning of a decision.

Decision instigators

In contrast to long-anticipated decisions, some spring into the world without lengthy deliberation. Those that apparently bypass conscious planning often accompany "discoveries." Frequently something long sought (perhaps unconsciously) is stumbled across in the course of pursuing other aims: the (wo)man of one's dreams walks into the lifeworld, the perfect solution to a problem is devised by others, or the job always desired is advertised. The career path of Edward Steichen, American photographer, exemplifies this. In his autobiography,

Steichen explains that he had been pursuing a career in painting, experimenting with fellow art students in Milwaukee, when the first exhibit of "photography as art" was held in another city:

> This was the first time that photographs had been shown in an art museum in America or, perhaps, anywhere. It was the most stimulating and exciting thing I had heard of in photography. Here was the knowledge that there were serious photographers at work in Europe and America, and that the oldest art museum in America was interested enough to exhibit their photographs.
>
> At the next session of the Art Students' League, I read this article (about the exhibit) to my fellow students, who were almost as much agog about it as I was. One of the girls piped up, "Why don't you send some of your photographs to the next exhibition?" The response was guffaws and giggles from some of the students, but then and there I made up my mind that if there ever was another such exhibition, I would submit some of my own photographs.
>
> (Steichen, 1963, n.p.)

"Then and there" he made up his mind, but not without having previously wished that photography could be an accepted art form. For this decision to be made so suddenly, a structure of unsatisfied intentions had to be already in place. Most deny this, preferring to be amazed at the suddenness of their choice. In Steichen's case, the choice actually had a long unconscious preparation in his previous artwork. Many times he had wished for a medium that would accomplish certain objectives not possible with paints. As soon as the possibility of realizing that desire became more than a vague dream, there was no cause for hesitation. A year later, on his way to Europe to study art, Steichen stopped in New York and met Steiglitz, a pioneer of photography as art, who teased the young Steichen. "Well, I suppose now that you're going to Paris, you'll forget about photography and devote yourself entirely to painting," he joked. "I will always stick to photography," Steichen shouted back. And so he did.

When a course of action seems both absolutely necessary and completely desirable, there is a tendency to forget, even to deny, that it could actually be serving other purposes. Steichen's eagerness to go to Europe to study photography, for example, may easily have been established by difficulties with his parents regarding his career choice. Quite commonly *the sense of excited compulsion accompanying an anticipated transformation of a life structure stems from what it is that one is getting out of and away from*, as much as it devolves from real qualities of the new situation.

An examination of the aspects of the new life structural elements which are most gleefully anticipated clearly symbolize the features of current or past life structures which one imagines will be transcended, almost magically, by the change. For example, Betsy was doing poorly in her job as a telephone operator, so to get out of it she applied to be a telephone lineman. It was unlikely that she would be accepted, being overweight and not energetic, but the idea appealed to her. She was attracted by the extra pay, the possibility of moving away from the town where her ex-husband lived, the status she would have for doing a man's job – all without considering the nature of the work she would have to do. This tendency to get lost in the attractive features of a possibility sets up a most common self-deception, colloquially known as "not seeing the forest for the trees."

Dilemmas

When the emergence of a possibility does not lead to an immediate plunge, it is usually because a dilemma is experienced. Logicians define a dilemma as the necessity of choosing between two equally *undesirable* alternatives. This state of affairs exists only in abstract logical problems. It rarely arises in real life (unless, for example, one were forced to choose one's mode of execution). Individuals often do choose to structure their dilemmas in this formal way, when in reality the alternatives are not *equally* undesirable. This set-up serves to justify indecision and forgives failure to make progress in deliberation. We will use the term dilemma to designate any major point of confused intentionality which seems to call for a decision.

It is said of some individuals that they create their own problems, that if they lacked a dilemma, they would make one up. To some extent, this is valid. All of us participate in constructing our own dilemmas. The contradictions between life spheres contribute to the emergence of a problem, but as we saw in the case of Bill (Chapter 6) it is possible to ignore both the origin of the problem and our interest in taking it on.

Here we will take a look at a number of dilemmas to understand some of the ways in which it could be said that we participate in constructing our own problems.

Any dilemma comes into awareness as a question posed to the self. These are of different sorts: What now? Where to? How do I get where I want to be? This way or that way? Each of the vignettes below portrays a dilemma that we can attempt to understand. Some readers might know with certainty what they would do in each of these situations, but the subjects involved were definitely perplexed. We will see why momentarily.

As an unmarried teenager, Laurie had to give up her daughter for adoption, but ironically ended up marrying the child's father. Now that she has had a son, she wishes she could get to know her daughter. Should she get in touch? Will her daughter want to know her?

Nathan has tried at least five diverse occupations in his 20 adult years. He is getting tired of switching around and would like to find something he could sink his teeth into. He finally decides that graduate study in linguistics will pull together his varied interests. After a month of classes, however, he is bored to death and feels compelled to drop out. He is depressed about his repeated false starts and is trying to decide what to do next.

Donna has two kids and has worked in a factory for five years since her divorce. She hates her job. Just as she was breaking up with a boyfriend, she became pregnant and decided to keep the baby. Now she wonders how she can possibly support another child and give it adequate care. She is on maternity leave and sees this as her chance to change her life, but can't decide which way to turn.

In expanding on each of these dilemmas, we will see how intimately dilemmas are linked to contexts beyond their immediate referents. Even though they have origins in life-structural complications, the fact that they become serious dilemmas depends on their relation to a life history. Laurie had really wanted to keep her daughter, but was forced to give her up by her boyfriend's parents. Her own parents stayed out of the picture, not wanting to get involved in the scandal (Laurie's father is a minister) and not understanding their daughter's need for support in her desire. This sense of not being cared for by her own parents may have triggered the teenage pregnancy in the first place (a common way of creating someone who needs you when you feel unwanted), but it serves now as a backdrop for Laurie's own desire to get in touch with her long-lost daughter. She says she would like to prove that she *does* care, but senses that her daughter would have a very hard time believing her, given the circumstances. In fact, the fear of rejection by her own daughter in the wake of rejection by the parents for embarrassing them might be too much to bear. Even this brief glance at the life-historical context of her dilemma shows why she is "stuck."

Nathan's dilemma reveals a persistent problem with achievement.

Many of his career changes occurred just as he was beginning to be comfortable and successful in an activity. We could speculate that this change, the decision to drop out of linguistics, occurs quickly because he is so much closer to achieving what he has always wanted – a career in writing. His dominating and uneducated father had difficulty tolerating Nathan's success in school. He forbade reading and writing in the house. Nathan read secretly at night and has spent much of his adulthood working toward publishing his written work. The degree in linguistics would have required writing and publishing in direct confrontation with the father's taboo. Again, we notice that a dilemma rests on considerations which go far beyond the immediate context of a person's decision. In Nathan's case, its recurrence is obvious, in contrast to Laurie's dilemma, which seems to have become an issue only in the wake of having given birth to a son.

Donna's dilemma, our third example, also has life-historical dimensions which make it more difficult than it may appear. In deciding to keep her surprise baby, she is repeating an act her mother made thirty years earlier. Donna's mother had two children early in her marriage, then decided not to have any more. Eight or ten years later, another child was conceived – Donna. Our interviews shows that for Donna, keeping this baby is part of beginning to accept herself. It has triggered a number of drastic life changes. Instead of going back to the factory after her maternity leave, she plans to get a college degree (on loans) and then pursue training in social work, specifically in order to help divorced women learn to cope. She sees this as living both for her daughter and belatedly for herself. She says she has a new vigor and zest in life now and realizes that if it were not for having to struggle with this very difficult dilemma she might never have extricated herself from the factory. Again a dilemma originates and is sustained in the matrix of a life history. Despite this historical embeddedness, these interviewees generally spoke only about the immediate or future aspects of the decision at hand. This is not surprising. The psychology of decision making itself generally sees deciding as a cognitive phenomenon designed only to manage a current problem.

Here a short review is in order. Husserl (1948), in his phenomenological description of judgment, indicates that dilemmas typically emerge when previously valid knowledge is contradicted in experience. This can happen when accepted ideas are reviewed or challenged, either by oneself or by another. In the case of life-structural transformations, these are rarely mere intellectual reorderings of the sort that Husserl acknowledges.

In a less cognitive, but still intellectualistic approach, Shainberg

(1973) describes life-structural and character change in an interesting book called *The Transforming Self*. Following Kuhn's analysis of scientific revolutions, Shainberg points out that personal crises or dilemmas can develop when two worldviews are in conflict. Each worldview seems to be an exclusive way of organizing one's goals and everyday activities. Shainberg's clinical experience teaches him that unless the conflict associated with a dilemma is great enough, existing life spheres will be elaborated to handle it, just as qualifications are made in a scientific theory to rescue it from disproof. A crisis in a life structure follows from the impending collapse of a life sphere. The changing individual tenses up in this battle of paradigms, relating many trivial events of the day to the issue being decided and even experiencing mild delusional states as old forms make their last claims for the person's loyalty. This is hardly a process which can be traced only as a chain of ideas as Shainberg's comparison to scientific world-views suggests. Dilemmas are *affective* structures grounded in aspects of social relations currently and historically experienced. "Ideas" represent these conflicts indirectly and succeed in managing those structures only partially.

For example, we saw that Mary (Chapter 2) tolerated occasional beatings from her husband on the assumption that this must be a fact of modern marriage. She had not seen her father hit her mother, but somehow sensed that she deserved brutal treatment herself. She started asking her friends if they were beaten by their husbands. All of them were horrified and urged Mary to do something about the situation. Although she understood that she was being abused, she was unable to make a change for several years. After divorcing her husband, she proceeded to marry another abusive man. Changes in ideas about life do not necessarily translate into changes in engagements or in one's character. It follows that dilemmas may not capture the real issue at hand, especially not as the individual first conceptualizes them.

A psychological analysis of decision making also risks ignoring a most powerful instigator of major life decisions: MONEY, usually the lack of it, but also sudden influxes, like inheritances, lottery winnings, loans. We have already seen, in Bill's case, the effect of finances on a stable life structure. Life changes rapidly evolve into life crises through the impact of financial matters, and finances are frequently used to rationalize changes when the actual reasons are unacceptable or unacknowledged.

This analysis of dilemmas and the origins of decisions would be entirely misleading if we failed to stress that all of these issues which provoke decisions are constituted interpersonally, that is, in a web of social relations where each subject's desires and intentions have an effect on the self-understandings of others. Nathan's jagged career path occurs in imaginary interactions with his father, Donna's decision to keep the baby and return to school is a message of allegiance to her mother. Laurie's search for her daughter speaks to her inlaws and to her own parents about their past errors. These communications are distorted because certain conflicting wishes are not directly expressed. Instead, an imaginary dialogue is carried on between the figures involved, making decisions more difficult, or at least, less determined by the subject's own primary desires.

Beyond the level of immediately significant figures in one's life history, dilemmas are also constructed in a larger sociocultural matrix. Laurie is well aware that new networks for tracing long-lost adopted children are being established and that social workers are trained to help patch up these relationships. Nathan has had his dose of propaganda about finding the career that fits your dreams and has probably read statistics showing that more and more people change careers frequently to carry out that search. Dilemmas are to a large extent socially provided. They are appropriated by individuals whose experiences in family, school, friendships, and other social relations have predisposed them to "resonate" with the contradictions contained in popular dilemmas. Grappling with a dilemma does not guarantee a positive resolution, however. The process of deciding determines the extent to which that can occur. Dilemmas cannot be accepted as self-justifying, but need to be considered as emblems of life processes that are not only situationally determined or restricted in their implications to a single sphere of life.

Framing

Tversky and Kahnemann (1981) show that the manner in which a problem is "framed" or conceptualized can drastically alter preferences for alternatives. They define a frame as

> the decision-maker's conception of the acts, outcomes, and contingencies associated with a particular choice. The frame that a decision-maker adopts is controlled partly by the formulation of the problem and partly by the norms, habits, and personal characteristics of the decision-maker. (Tversky and Kahnemann, 1981, p. 453)

This perspective leads the authors to conclude, after a number of studies testing the rationalistic expected-utility model, that rational choices are more probable when attention is given to alternative frames through which a problem could be conceptualized than when a decision is made within the first frame that suggests itself.

To accept this conclusion and to say no more would deny a primary insight to be had from the study of narrative accounts of decision making.

Framing fixes the issue to be decided in a specific form. This moment is rarely questioned. It always seems obvious that what is to be decided *has* to be decided. The movement toward the framing of a decision usually occurs unconsciously during our initial attempts to conceptualize the dilemma we are facing. After that point, we have enough on our hands and therefore do all we can to keep matters simple, especially if the decision-as-framed is a tough one. Unfortunately, the process of framing can serve to close our eyes to less drastic solutions and cuts off numerous possibilities, alternatives, strategies, or compromises. We end up deciding with a limited grasp of our situation thanks to the framing process. On the other hand, framing can place us in a world much more complex than it actually needs to be and may even completely misrepresent a problem.

Framing a decision is like taking aim. It determines which spheres of the life structure are targeted for change. Compare the framing of these two decisions:

I want to decide where in the Western United States I should live.

I want to decide whether to live in Boulder or Berkeley.

These examples show us that frames shape not only the target of a decision (where to live) but the breadth of fire (range of locations considered). The difference holds for other types of decisions as well:

What kind of artist should I be?

Should I be a painter or a sculptor?

Because numerous possibilities are excluded for every inch of narrowness in decision frames, it would seem crucial to challenge the framing which initially comes to mind when confronted with a dilemma. It may inadvertently ignore real opportunities or even intentionally screen off the best solution.

This much may be obvious. What seems to be widely ignored is that one can call into question and attempt to understand the urgent sense of needing to decide within a certain frame. In too many situations, a decision to change the life structure is framed prematurely and unnecessarily.

A phenomenological study of the emergence of a decision frame accounts only partially for the urge to adopt the decision mentality. We should, however, consider this experience briefly: When one is confronted with a complex dilemma in a life sphere a variety of mental states are evoked. Anxieties, fears, summonings of courage and determination, fantasies of ideal outcomes, denials of problems, images of possible strategies, and anticipations of others' reactions vie for attention. The more openly one faces the dilemma, the more contradictions emerge. One aspect of the self after another is called into question and the entire set of assumptions underlying involvement in a life sphere can crumble away. A way to shut down the dizzying complexity of the train of thought is sought and grabbed as soon as it offers itself. The urge to "decide one thing at a time" sets in and a frame is adopted as if it were a cap for a geyser – steam only pushes through where there is a crack in the earth – or a dam constructed to stop the flood of contrasts and self-contradictions. The framed decision carves out a manageable realm of confusion.

This analysis makes clear the fact that multiple contradictory intentions pre-exist the framing of a choice and that these jostle for representation. If this is so, I propose that Freud's (1900) model for the interpretation of dreams could serve for the "decoding" of a decision frame. In other words, the frame potentially expresses more than the intentions immediately captured in its structure. Even when a frame is broad and simply formulated it says more than it seems to. A key to unraveling its code is to take the choice of words used to capture the dilemma very seriously.

The following analysis of Karen's decision dilemma will exemplify this method of decoding.

Karen volunteered to be interviewed a few weeks after she had decided to move away from Lansing to spend a year traveling in order to "find a place to settle down." Karen was 25, had been married for a few years, then divorced. At that time she moved to Lansing and took a job as a commercial artist. She enjoyed her job quite a lot, but after two years began to feel the urge to move to another part of the country.

Having sold most of her heavy possessions, Karen planned to head west to Colorado and then move north and south as she worked her way further west. Ideally she would spend a year traveling, staying for a couple of weeks in any town that appealed to her, meeting the people, checking out the opportunities and general lifestyle. This would tell her if she would "enjoy living there." Her goal was to "find a place to settle down, buy a house . . . until something else comes up." Intuition would tell her when she had come across the right place. This was expressed in a queer phrase about going out west on the "presumption of where I would like to live. I'll know when I'm there." She had that feeling when she first moved to Lansing, but it turned out to be too cold in the winter there.

Off-handedly, Karen mentioned that her mother had recently moved to Santa Barbara and had asked Karen to move there, too. She refused, "Maybe Santa Fe or Phoenix. They're better for allergies." We have indications already that her strategy is linked both to health issues and to relational ties.

I asked her what led up to this urge to pull up all the stakes to move west (she was raised in Michigan):

> I went east last fall for three weeks. I have to go someplace every three months. I have to travel and do things while I'm young. My sister committed suicide in July. On my trip I went through mourning. That inspired me to get out and live.
>
> Now that I have the money, I want to get out, see new things. I prefer to travel with my money, rather than spend it on everyday living. It clears my head. I have to move around. And it's not that I'm getting away from work, but that I'm going somewhere else. I can just follow my own urges with no prohibitions. I don't need a lot of rules or roles. I can move and easily get out. I grow when I move, whether it's jobs or relationships.

What does staying in one place mean to you then?

> I move every year lately. My parents are divorced, so there's some instability there. I would like to have a house to stay in permanently. . . . I don't like the idea of not having a home. What if I end up like another Flying Dutchman, destined to roam from city to city?

Given that she is setting up exactly that, it seems we need to understand this glaring contradiction more. She is searching for a place to settle down, but knows that she has to keep moving to grow. Here's a first stab at making sense of this: Karen is trying to recreate a sense of having a home, but given that her marriage has broken up, her parents have separated, her sister is no longer around, and she is unhealthy in her home state, she feels she should make her own home somewhere else. At some level, going toward her mother and to a warmer climate makes sense, but she doesn't know how far to go. She has been deceived too many times already. She refuses to be fooled again, but still longs for security. The contradiction shows up again in her next response:

Do you have any doubts about your strategy for deciding where to live?

Well, um. . . . Only when I worry about aimlessness. I could deceive myself about where to live. I could lose my self-assurance if I get aimless. And I wonder if I can be happy being settled down in one place for too long.

I wanted to know more about Karen's relationship with her mother. It seemed that the desire to bounce around the west betrayed a sense that none of those places would be good enough – that she really wanted to be in Santa Barbara with her mother, but something holds her back.

What about moving to Santa Barbara to be close to your mother?

We have a close relationship and I also have other relatives there, but I need to talk to my mother about what she wants from me. She's about to retire and I don't want to get involved in taking care of her. . . .
    She admitted to me that I didn't get much as a kid, that I was short-changed, but now I'm trying to break away from the apron strings. We're friends, but we'll never lose track of the mother-daughter thing. Still I would consider moving in that direction; I'd be interested in being closer. . . .

To cash in on what she offers you now?

I don't want to be a kid again. I don't want to get smothered.

Apparently Karen is afraid to get *too* close to her mother and will have to search for awhile to find the appropriate geographical/emotional distance. The fact that Karen has ruled out living in the east confirms her claim about wanting to be closer than she is now. We are beginning to understand a part of Karen's concern about where to live, but there is another level to this dilemma that provokes her decision to be framed both as a question of where to live *and* of where she would *enjoy living*.
    In probing to understand this, I asked her if there were other factors that played a part in her decision to move.

Health. My sister's health, okay? My dad's health. He had a serious operation a year ago. Weird things can happen. My brother has a collapsed lung occasionally. You just never know what will happen.
    I used to worry about going blind, because my eyes went bad very quickly. I worry about not having control over things, over my health.

I would *kick* myself if I didn't go now. I can't imagine myself as sedentary. I see myself as lively.

Is she saying that she would *kill* herself if she didn't make a move now? She does seem very concerned with death.

I can't do things like mountain climbing forever, so I should do it now. I feel like I have a vibrant self when I put myself to the test. When I'm at the top of a mountain after hand-over-hand climbing, it's very exhilarating. I love it. I'm at my fullest.

The top of a mountain is about as far as you can get from being six feet under. I asked her what that full feeling is contrasted to in her experiences.

My job. It keeps me sitting down. Most health problems have to do with lack of exercise. My blood runs slow. I get sluggish. I have more energy if I've been doing things. I feel more mentally fit when I exercise more. I need to keep the ball rolling. When I see people who look strong I admire them. Since I told my boss I was quitting I have lots of energy. I feel free. I can do what I want.

I know a lot of people who never left their own town. A growing person does a lot of things and isn't afraid to try something new. I'll do something just because I haven't done it before, but I won't take a dangerous risk. I guess I really value life. I can tie this in to my sister's suicide. I used to be suicidal, but I got out of it finally, and got stronger for having got rid of those feelings.

Clearly, Karen's question is not only about where to live – it is about how to *live*, how to stay alive. She frames her question as she does in order to avoid suicidal imagery and to push herself to set up a new life structure which will help her to enjoy life more, to fend off feelings of loss and sadness that inevitably well up when she is sedentary. We now see why she worries about settling down, but at the same time fears that she might get too tired if she stays on the road. What is interesting about the way she has framed her decision is that no matter how she answers it, she has excluded the alternative she fears most – staying in one place and being sedentary. When she talks about what she will do with her time out west, she conjures up active images of white water rafting and mountain climbing (although probably she will end up sitting around a lot of hotels, restaurants, theatres, and resorts).

If Karen finally decides where to live, it is likely to be based on a feeling that even if she settles there, she will be forced by the local lifestyle to get out, to move, and grow.

Decision frames pretend to have the goal of "coming to terms" with reality, but can accomplish just the opposite. The depression Karen struggles with is likely to creep back any time she gets tired or lonely, no matter where she lives. Some other sort of confrontation with those feelings, allowing her to come to grips with her personal history, might help her to be able to settle down and have the home she wants. As Freud says, "every neurosis has the result, and therefore probably the purpose, of forcing the patient out of real life, of alienating him from actuality" (1911, p. 213). Much of this alienation is furthered by the manner in which we take hold of our dilemmas.

Another subject managed to find a way around a framing problem. She was about to graduate from college and was faced with the common decision between following her boyfriend as he pursued his career goals or pursuing her own. She seemed to have a good chance of getting an internship which would prepare her to do investigative journalism. Her older sister, much admired by the father, had taken the career route, passing up the only man she ever really enjoyed. She is now successful but quite unhappy in her personal life. Fearing the same outcome, my interviewee struggled to find a compromise frame to decide within. She didn't want it to be a choice between being with her boyfriend and pursuing her career. The possibility of seeing it otherwise was restricted by the fact that his law school was located in a place with very little opportunity for a beginning in journalism. The dilemma was finally framed as a problem of needing to know if the relationship was a sound one. The woman decided to accompany her boyfriend, but not to live with him, and even bought a trailer home in case she needed to make a quick escape.

In counseling settings, one repeatedly sees clients who come in thinking they *just have to* decide whether to do X or Y, whether it be to stay in school or drop out, to transfer to another school or stay there, to break up with so-and-so or get married, to get divorced or not, to be an artist or a mechanic. Inevitably, these dichotomies can be interpreted as smokescreens masking more important issues, self-doubts, or dilemmas.

Often the alternatives posed are constructed in a manner which precludes the possibility of deciding anything. A woman who was about to graduate from college told me that she really did not know what to do. She thought she would either move to Nicaragua to help rebuild the strife-torn country – she speaks Spanish fluently – or stay here in the United States to hold on to the house she has maintained payments on only with great difficulty while she put herself through school. Staying here, though, would be impossible because she refuses to do a "shit job" ever again and "knows" there are no good jobs. Simultaneously, going to Nicaragua would be impossible because she cannot fathom leaving her house. She thinks she'll never have the means to buy one again. Moreover, if she goes to Nicaragua for a couple of years, she would be no better off when she came back than she is now. The stalemate allows her to remain indecisive and will probably force her to collect welfare for many months until something comes up to save her from the mess she is in (e.g., a marriage proposal, an inheritance, or some other external rescuer).

Decision conflicts in which two alternatives are mutually exclusive (often some compromise is possible but not wanted) have interesting properties. The characterological origin of conflict heightens the tendency for alternatives to be suspended in a meaningful relation to each other; they "speak" to each other. In the case of the woman who wanted to go to Nicaragua, the tension between the two poles may represent a characterological (and social) struggle between activity (revolutionary change) and passivity (traditional American home-maker). The life-structural perspective on decisions leads one to adopt a skeptical stance toward the compulsion to decide. The more one feels one must decide, the more it is likely that the choice would be constrained by attempts to resolve unacknowledged deeper issues which will hardly be addressed through a life-structural change.

Everyday life and the course of deliberation

When a person has a decision to make, it appears that associated deliberation occurs at odd moments, perhaps when there is a break in a routine or as one is going to sleep. The decision is like a puzzle retrieved from a drawer for yet another attempt at a solution. To view delibera-tion as self-enclosed in this manner is to overlook a number of insights suggested by the principle of psychic determinism. Attention is not simply drawn toward the dilemma for lack of anything else to do. The decision problem generally re-emerges because it coincides with a particular mood, event, conversation, theme, symbol, or desire experi-enced in preceding moments. One is *reminded* of the need to decide by something in the practical world, in everyday life.

The power of minor involvements to trigger deliberation derives from their capacity to represent in concrete form an aspect of the conflict at hand. Bill, for example, reported wondering whether to take on a part-time job to earn more money as he drove to work amidst scores of cars newer and shinier than his own. Sometimes it seems that the decider seeks clues or omens as to how to decide. The symbolic power of objects and events lies in the interaction between the subject's confused intentions and the world. One looks to the world for answers. If one is deciding which route up a mountain would be safer, this strategy is, of course, natural. In the case of major life decisions, however, the perceived world provides no meaningful help. The symbols or omens we find in it are not arbitrary, but are projections of our own inclinations. The scientific age has not cured us of superstitions, particularly in the realm of decisions. Good weather becomes an omen that one should go ahead with a commitment. A sprained ankle is taken as a sign that one was not meant to travel. One bad grade in school can shift a person's interest significantly. We joke about these tendencies but the fact that such ideas come to mind is a clue that similar processes are operative even when we are seriously deliberating.

Other people also serve to instigate deliberation. An individual may have tucked a dilemma away, hoping not to have to face it for a while, only to have a friend ask, "Have you decided yet?" Some characters are predisposed to rely entirely on intersubjectively prompted deliberation to carry out their decision making. Many decisions are handed over to a person by others who are able to sensitize them to a dilemma. A common example would be the career choice installed in a child's mind by early attempts to answer incessant adult questions about "What are you going to be when you grow up?" And, in adulthood, certain sadistically inclined individuals enjoy opening up anxieties in acquaintances by showing how the latter's solid assumptions in a decision are not tenable.

Other factors of everyday life, such as fatigue, time of day, deadlines, other pressing responsibilities, horoscopes, articles or books chanced upon, accidents, and so on, can enter into the process of deliberation in the most irrational ways. The best one can do is to watch for these effects and to interpret them as signs of intentions which may not be finding expression in the more "logical" moments.

Positioning at the moment of choice

The meaning of important life choices, particularly those which directly involve the formation or rupture of intimate bonds, can often be interpreted through an analysis of the situation in which the decision is finally made. By "situation," I mean a wide range of potentially meaningful characteristics of the lifeworld, e.g., proximity to the persons or projects involved in the change, time of day, degree of development of project, familiarity of setting, mood, and so forth.

Decisions about which there is a great deal of intrapsychic or inter-personal conflict may require a certain constellation of elements to fall into place before a closure of deliberation can be achieved.

An interesting case which illustrates the present point was related by Sarah, 32, who described her decision to remarry. In the week prior to that decision, Sarah had become increasingly disillusioned by her involvement with a certain lover. She resolved to break up with him and packed up all the things he had left at her apartment. That weekend she loaded her car, drove to his house, and returned his possessions, telling him that she would prefer not to see him anymore. They argued for a while about the break-up, then, in a complete reversal of her intent, Sarah proposed marriage.

An interpretive analysis of this incident in conjunction with seven other interviews supports the conclusion that a number of relatively trivial circumstances combined to set the stage for an enactment of a drama of sorts on that day. The meaning-laden trivia included the fact that he asked her to help him erect a radio antenna on his roof, that she sat below him on the ground while he sat in a chair, and so forth.

The general point to be made here is that thematic similarities between contemporary and past scenes require props. A script is insufficient. Another actor has to be involved, even if absent from the stage. It is not a matter of imagination alone. Deliberation uses the crutches provided by actual situations to support its conclusions. Sarah's choice came about when an equation of her lover and her father (sorry, but it is clearly the case) occurred as she was trying to break up. She repeatedly told me that her father was like god to her and also described her lover's sunlit hair as godly. Her sense of submission to him repeated fondly remembered scenes of struggle with her father.

Only the beginning of this sort of investigation can be presented here. It is surprising to discover that moments of choice could be interpreted so clearly. But when one thinks about it, it becomes clear why this is so. When a decision is hard to make, it will take some sort of external "pressure" to get the ambivalent person over the threshold. Something has to happen. If thought alone has failed to come up with a solution, an outside impetus will be needed. The phenomenon is comparable to the concept of "day residue" which Freud (1900) articulates in trying to show why certain impressions from the day preceding a dream are selected for representation in the dream. Usually, some object elicited a wish which was not deemed acceptable at the time. That wish parallels an infantile wish which manages to achieve further expression in the dream. A choice relies on "day residue" in the same manner. We examine this sort of phenomenon in more depth in Chapter 8 when the concept of an "object-relational stereotype" is elaborated.

Adults in transit

The sheer frequency of life-structural transformation in modern life has given rise to a new psychology of transition making. This field has developed on the foundation of extensive research on coping mechanisms and adaptation to stress (Schlossberg, 1981). This literature is ahistorical: it sees a transition as self-enclosed, as a period to be dealt with well and then transcended. Another trend seeks to link transitions and "life crises" to certain ages, stages, phases, and other normative categories, as if to imply that these junctures are predictable or even inevitable (Levinson, 1978; Atchley, 1975). This literature is historical, but it attempts to standardize personal histories. We can assert that hardly any transitions are inevitable and those set up by decisions are never absolutely necessary.

A recent work, *Transitions*, by William Bridges (1982) provides a number of useful tips for managing transitions but falls into an untenable position which portrays transition as the natural process of disorientation and reorientation that marks the turning points of the path of growth.

> Throughout nature, growth involves periodic accelerations and transformations: things go slowly for a time and nothing seems to change – until suddenly the eggshell cracks, the branch blossoms, the tadpole's tail shrinks away, the leaf falls, the bird molts, the hibernation begins. With us it is the same. Although the signs are less clear than in the world of feather and leaf, the functions of transition times are the same. They are key times in the natural process of self-renewal. (Bridges, 1982, p. 5)

It is curious that these gushy remarks are prefaced by an account of the rapid social changes which make transitions more frequent and difficult. Humanistic psychologies are generally flawed by their attempt to attribute processes of "growth" to "natural" forces. In our study of decision narrative, it is increasingly clear that growth results from experience in interaction and self-reflection. The person left to rely on natural, inner growth processes will often take the turn toward addiction, masochism, or suicide in the midst of transition periods. In short, surrendering growth to "nature" empowers "character."

One could not deny that the recent attention to normative transitions is helping individuals pass through them more resourcefully. It seems, however, that many take the social science gospel too much to heart. People now worry if they have not passed through a mandated transition and sometimes define themselves as being in crisis for no good reason. Among young adults, in particular, it is becoming the mode to be always in transition, on the way to something else, "just passing through," stranded between a particular undesirable past and a bright, but vague future. This seems to be an attempt to deny the continuity of one's difficulties across the life structures one has set up.

The literature on coping does support the contention that a decision is designed to *negotiate* a life-structural transformation, not only to instigate it. In other words, the decision, as we have argued, implies more than a project to be carried out, but involves a shift in relations to self and others, to values, goals, and one's past. The ramifications a decision carries are demonstrated in analyses of the psychological stages typically associated with transitions. Models of "coping" reveal that decisions which change life structures are stretched out over long periods and pass through many psychological phases, each of which bears a different relation to the subject's dilemma and personal history. We can run through these typical phases, drawing on the general "transition process model" advanced by Hopson and Adams (in Brammer and Abrego, 1981). In their synthesis, the stages of a transition are:

1 shock and immobilization
2 denial
3 depression
4 letting go
5 testing options
6 search for meaning
7 integration.

Each of these phases points to an aspect of decision making as well as to ways of coping with transitions. Their relation to deciding is commonly ignored because it is assumed that a decision is completed as soon as it is made. In actuality, the decision process continues even after the conscious experience of having made a decision. The meaning of a decision depends as much on its aftermath as on factors and considerations that lead to it. Furthermore, the initial decision to change, as Husserl's analysis suggested, may only block out an area to be filled in later, during a transition phase, by decisions which serve to specify the intentions underlying the initial decision. The first phase only announces, "I'll go for this!" or "No more of that!" The transition phase serves to find answers to the question, "Now what?"

This notion seems to run counter to the psychoanalytic claim that understanding is precluded by the fact of deciding. This contradiction stems from confusing two contexts of a decision's meaning. The psychoanalytic injunction is to put off deciding until the characterological or life-historical contribution to the impulse to decide is understood and, ideally, consciously acknowledged and appropriated. In this section, we are concerned with another context of a decision's meaning, in particular, the more immediate and practical desires motivating decisions to modify, dismantle, or construct spheres of the life structure. Some of these intentions are manifest and accessible at the point of commitment to change, but others are revealed only later.

The "transition process model" serves as an outline of stages in which these meanings become clarified. The "shock and immobilization" following a decision may be minimal, but a feeling of being stunned or surprised by that to which one has just committed oneself is common. The accompanying affective discharge may be either elation or despair. This is not a blind discharge. It has an object – either a person or a project which is tangled in meanings for the self and others. The compromise by which the divided self was unified in decision required a surrender of something in order to gain other things. To suppress the potential conflict over losses, "denial" (stage 2) sets in. The initial overwhelming feelings are moderated. One sees this in people who downplay their excitement or who avoid admitting sadness or anger over a life change. The subsequent "depression" stage could be understood as a consequence of this denial, but is also due to realizations that certain cherished involvements will be disrupted and that some problems will not be alleviated by the coming change. Underlying these primarily cognitive processes, one can assume that a reworking of interpersonal attachments is taking place with regard to both current and past relationships. These reorderings are evidenced consciously in questions like, "How will my parents react to this news?" "How can I ever admit this to so-and-so?" or "Won't my grandparents be thrilled?"

The "letting go" stage involves a type of mourning over projects or aspects of relationships which had to be left behind or curtailed. Quite commonly, transitional substitutes are sought to make the separation easier. If unavailable, vows may be made to oneself in order to compensate ("I hate to leave California, but I swear I will come back for at least one visit each year.").

The search for substitutes plays an important role, usually from behind the back of the changing person, in the next phase, "testing options." This is only rarely a calm and rational time. Some individuals in transition hunger for solid ground, enter into new relationships impulsively, take up new projects haphazardly, and develop fantastic schemes. False starts and abrupt endings are painfully numerous in this phase, but gradually the "dream" which sought actualization through the momentous decision to change becomes clearer. People who have gone through this process repeatedly often hang back from new involvements not wanting to repeat mistakes and fearing unfamiliar situations.

The next stage, "search for meaning," incorporates reflection on the circumstances which brought about the change. A partial, typically shallow, understanding of the choice is constructed in light of its complex aftermath. Reasons for the decision may be radically revised ("I thought I was just frustrated with the situation, but I was actually trying to make a major change toward something entirely different. My boss tried to convince me that *I* wanted to leave, but now I see that he really wanted to get rid of me"). Such reformulations are compensatory in most cases. They serve to rebuild self-esteem, sidestep guilt, punish oneself for losses, or rationalize the inevitable. The value changes frequently observed at this stage (e.g., a new depth of concern for others, renewed religiosity, interest in autonomy) are typically only the external manifestation of deeper characterological development which can accompany or even stimulate major life changes. There is, however, a greater impetus to reflect, to take a "long hard look" at motives underlying past activities and desired goals.

Composing the new life structure

The final stage of the transition process, "integration," parallels the establishment of a new life structure. For the more self-reflective individual, this entails a form of "composition" not unlike musical or literary endeavors. A plotting, planning, and schematizing takes place in conjunction with extensive imaginative self-projection and commitment to a pattern of commitments, to a new lifestyle. The composer draws on understandings about where things went wrong in previous life structures, what was missing, and what deserves continuation or preservation. Themes of the new lifestyle may be boldly presented to others, just as Beethoven announces his thematic intentions early in a symphony.

At the christening of a new life structure, some imagine themselves to be in a new zone of freedom. This phase is actually highly constrained, however free the changing person may feel. In fact, one could venture that an examination of the actions which seem to feel most free at these times would find them to be the most compelled. This can be understood through a look at strategies undertaken by people entering this compositional phase.

Bearing in mind my assertion that the establishment of a new life structure sheds light on the issues which brought about the decision to change, a number of compositional styles can be noted. Some try to make as clean a break as possible with the past. Old friends are not seen. New social networks are sought. Memory-laden possessions are discarded. Different sports and hobbies are considered. Each of these moves is couched in a meaningful relation to the past, however. The total break may hint at the difficulty of separation from persons and projects. For example, Karen, in her search for a new place to live, is looking for a community exactly like the one she has chosen to leave. Similarly the hobby a young man took up after leaving his wife was one she would never have tolerated.

In contrast to this style, others seek to maintain or re-establish as many spheres of the previous life structure as possible. After moving to a new city, for example, some individuals immediately contact local organizations (church, political party, club, charge accounts) to which their "identity" is connected. Some of this need for continuity seems to be satisfied by dragging around souvenirs of previous life structures, however inconvenient.

An unfortunate but hardly avoidable style of composition is to *overcompensate* for the defects of the previous structure, to move from being too bored to being exhausted, from impoverishment to an overemphasis on money matters, from being too "out of it" to trying to be too "with it." Sarah, the woman who reversed her decision to break up with her lover, moved from a dangerously exciting first marriage (like her father, her first husband was abusive – on one occasion invited a bunch of motorcycle hoods to gang-rape Sarah) to a dull but safe marriage (Sarah reports having to dream up aggressive strategies to make sex exciting and was toying with the idea of having an affair). Overcompensation could be understood as being triggered by knowing for sure what one does *not* want and thus running full steam toward its thematic opposite, overshooting the happy medium.

A few subjects in transition told me of plans to reinstate projects or relationships which had to be abandoned at some point prior to the most recent life structures. This seemed to be a way of picking up the pieces of oneself in order to fashion a new identity. In the process, past involvements are scanned in search of satisfying activities which could be projected into the future. This creates a sense of continuity to counter the experience of rupture which accompanies any change. For young adults, this process frequently involves a reinvestment in a project that was encouraged by parents, then rebelled against, only to be taken up later as one's own: "Before, I did it for my parents; I choose it freely now." For older adults, such re-engagement could be a strategy for regaining a youthful feeling.

Regardless of compositional style, certain feelings seem to be unavoidable in composing the new life structure. First, there is a sense of a "golden beginning," a "rebirth," a "nirvana" feeling. Psychoanalytic authors link this state to the acting out which is made possible by the decision to change. The psychic tension of the dilemma phase is eased after the break with the recent past is accomplished. The image of what lies ahead remains glowing in idealized form on the foundation of experiences in the distant past. This fresh start at the threshold of a new life sphere is not unlike an infatuation. It will typically fade as it is battered by actuality. The grass is rarely greener. The self cannot be left behind. The accomplished work takes on a life of its own and is not what one intended it to be.

These considerations lead one to conclude that an awareness of the ways in which one is bound by past life structures, even recent ones, would contribute more to personal freedom from constraints of the past than strategies which symbolically break with the past but actually serve to carry it forward.

Limitations of life-structural reflection

What manner of reflection made it possible to advance the foregoing points? Basically, I have noted how the immediate and practical involvements which make up a life structure push one toward the necessity of deciding (or fend it off), contribute to the course of deliberation, and are eventually modified as a result of the decision to change. The forces involved in these processes are not susceptible to quantification or measurement, but they exert a *real* effect. The mediations between practical matters and the course of the deciding consciousness create a symbolic order in which actions are carried out. That order consists of historically molded representations which guide one's involvements. The effects of this reality derive from the emotional weight of commitments, shared histories, the clash of goals, the fear or thrill of violence, even sheer boredom.

Decisions turn out to be much more than the purely subjective operations described by phenomenologists or cognitive psychologists. Decisions are points of impact, confrontation, surrender, and struggle against situations.

The limitations of the life-structural perspective are evident from the fact that in considering the practical origins of dilemmas and the immediate precipitants of choices, among other things, we found repeatedly that these factors were only significant because of their life-historical and social contexts. The life-structural context opens up on to these other contexts in every sphere. As this is the case, we have to argue that a life-structural perspective on decision making, while it complements extant views of the process, is insufficient. It is either too vague, offering no indications of where important linkages might be found, or too narrow, in that it can easily be taken to include only the current concerns of the subject.

A final point needs to be made to stave off a potential misunderstanding. Because our attention is focused on decisions which set up life-structural transformations, we have ignored a type of decision which is equally important. We hardly consider these decisions because they make no apparent difference in the life-structure. I refer to the repetitive recommitment to one's projects and relationships. Daily, weekly, yearly, frustration can induce hesitation and self-examination. Can I go on? Is this worth doing? Does anyone appreciate my efforts? The most difficult decisions for some individuals may result in little change in the outward appearance of their lives, but make possible the reassertion and reaffirmation of a goal, or recommitment to an ideal, which has equal claim, if not more, to the title "decision."

A cruel paradox of life is that it is difficult to ascertain whether renewed dedication to a project is exactly what it will take to bring it to fruition or if it would be masochistic, even stupid, to continue. The narcissistic cultural trends of today clearly favor giving up when the going gets tough, aiming for the quick pay-off, and moving to more fertile ground. But a counterrationale advocates holding on to what one has, limiting "unrealistic" expectations, and working within a situation to make continued involvement more rewarding.

Part of the solution to this paradox becomes evident when we correct a deficiency of both the life-structural and life-historical perspectives. Because they take the individual as the "unit of analysis," decisions to change life structures appear to be isolated from social structures. The latter are, of course, composed of interdependent life structures. We live in collectivities. Our activities are intertwined with those of others. Any question about the ideal composition of a life-structure refers implicitly to changes in social action as well as to potential developments of one's character. The two poles, character and society, are in the final analysis so irrevocably intertwined that to imagine change in one without altering the other is wishful thinking.

LIFE PROJECTS

The new "life-span" psychologies have managed to take us beyond ridiculous worries about whether or not there is psychological development during adulthood. Now we find a multitude of theories about adult development, each clamoring for attention among popular psychology trade books and in respected journals.

The essential feature of most of these models lies in the conceptualization of the adult life course as a *series* of stages, levels, issues, or problems. To accomplish this feat of abstraction, a theorist has to stand back from the individual life to grasp the commonalities across persons and their lives. This body of research and theory definitely provides a form of enlightenment to the individual naively proceeding into and through adulthood, but has severe limitations which come to light as one examines the role of major decisions in relation to personality development.

No "Seasons of a Man's Life"

These limitations derive from the external standpoint taken up by the theorists of adult development. The attempt to impose a conceptual framework of stages, issues, or crises on the individual life nearly automatically excludes consideration of the life-historical and life-structural contexts of life choices. Once these meaning-conferring

contexts are neglected, any discussion of change becomes irrelevant –
change in relation to what? To what purpose?

This critique could be developed for any of the currently popular
models – particularly as they trickle down into psychology textbooks or
popular works: White's *Lives in Progress* (1952), Erikson's *Childhood
and Society* (1963), Loevinger's *Ego Development* (1976), Gould's
Transformations (1978), to name but a few.

Robert White's *Lives in Progress* (1952) provides a clear example of
the insufficiency of the *naturalistic* perspective which hampers most
contemporary models of life-span development.

The subtitle of the book is "A Study of the *Natural* Growth of
Personality." White claims that, historically, directions of growth
after the attainment of biological maturity have been defined in ethical
terms. In recent years, however, thanks to the advances of psychological and social science, we can now understand these growth trends
through reference to a "naturalistic system" (1952, p. 331). What
growth trends occur in such a way that they can be best understood as
natural processes? Let us examine these in turn.

1   Stability of ego identity: As one moves into and through adult-
    hood, "accumulated experience . . . more and more outweighs the
    impact of new events" (White, 1952, p. 338). This contributes to
    the solidification of a sense of self, to consistency of action, and to
    greater effectiveness. Obviously the primary accomplishments in
    this trend are achieved through the assumption of adult roles in an
    occupation, family, community. But the assumption of those roles
    is hardly a natural process – it involves decisions, practical experi-
    ence, coincidences, compromises, disillusionment, and a number of
    other not-so-natural occurrences. So much White admits as he
    describes his cases, contradicting the theoretical view he proposes.

2   Freeing of personal relationships: This trend encompasses the
    increased ability to see another person for what he/she actually is,
    enhanced empathic powers, and interpersonal assertiveness. Two
    factors contributing to such growth are unanticipated: "shocking"
    reactions from others and alterations in one's social environment
    (moving, absences, new friends). Again, these are far from being
    naturally produced changes, but rely on social, economic, and
    cultural events and configurations.

3   Deepening of interests: This trend is basically characterized by
    greater commitment to specific, realistic actions as idealistic dreams
    and fantasies are tempered by experience. What are the so-called

natural processes which lead to the deepening of interests? Social support, emergence of opportunities for the expression of interests, the unification of several divergent interests, and the satisfying consequences of early accomplishments. Even the last of these processes definitely occurs in a social field which can hardly be seen as naturally constituted. Societies typically manage to make individuals feel good about doing the things that contribute to the maintenance or reproduction of existing institutions.

4   Humanizing of values: Abstract and idealistically advanced values become "personalized" as experience fills them out and their purposes are clarified. A personal philosophy of life develops from the conflict of values within oneself and with others. In what sense can this process be said to be natural? It only appears to occur naturally because we do not pay much attention to the manner in which it proceeds. Any careful examination of the origins of value systems will determine that they serve particular interests, both character-based and culturally functional, which can hardly be said to be dictated by nature (Geuss, 1981).

5   Expansion of caring: Adults, in general become "generative" (Erikson) and display greater "social interest" (Adler). This stems from a growing awareness of what it takes to make society work, from parenting, and realizing that others have needs that can be met without sacrificing one's own needs. Apart from the biological process of childbearing involved here, these realizations involve social experiences, saturated with social meanings, not mere natural processes.

I have stressed this point to counter a trend in humanistic psychology (especially in Maslow and Rogers) which sees growth as something that occurs wonderfully on its own, as a tree shoots out limbs or a lion comes to be King of the Jungle. White adopted this jargon of naturalism and stressed the "healthy," "positive" movements of development, but the examples he gives of experiences which lead to growth often do not "naturally" produce real growth. For many individuals, these growth trends are blocked by oppressive social arrangements or unfortunate experiences in socializing institutions. The outcome is rarely ideal and the synthesis achieved seems most likely to be a compromise with social conditions, rather than an ethically or aesthetically pleasing achievement. Similar critiques could be developed for each of the popular humanistic models of development.

Radical perspectives

What are the alternatives to naturalistic and normative models of adult development? Three contemporary views come much closer to addressing the questions we will pose regarding the role of major decisions in adult life. Not surprisingly, these authors are more familiar with the implications of continental philosophy and psychoanalysis.

In his perceptive *Boundaries*, Robert Lifton argues that we need to depart radically from usage of terms like "character" and "personality," in order to "grasp the even more significant elements of change and flux which characterize not only our external environment but our inner experience" (1969, p. 37). He argues that the concept of the Protean man, one who shifts shape with ease, is appropriate to modern psychological styles:

> the protean style of self-process, then, is characterized by an interminable series of experiments and explorations, some shallow, some profound, each of which can readily be abandoned in favor of still new, psychological questions. This pattern resembles, in many ways, what Erik Erikson has called "identity diffusion" or "identity confusion," and the impaired psychological functioning which these terms suggest can be very much present. But I want to stress that this protean style is by no means pathological as such, and in fact may be one of the functional patterns necessary to life in our times. I would emphasize that it extends to all areas of human experience – to political as well as to sexual behavior, to the holding and promulgating of ideas, and to the general organization of judgments concerning what is psychologically disturbed or pathological, as opposed to adaptive or even innovative.   (Lifton, 1969, p. 45)

Lifton seems to be arguing for a chameleon-like adaptation to the divergent roles we are required to play. This is quite a departure from the wisdom embodied in the western tradition, as in Goethe's encouragement to bring a unified self to bear on one's projects, to struggle to avoid compromising the core of one's personality.

David Cooper, colleague of R. D. Laing, offers a view which challenges Lifton's sense of the discontinuity of adult roles:

> if one sees one's life as a linear trajectory – out of some past, through the present, heading towards a future – one may be deluded . . . into conceiving that there is a goal at some ultimate point on this line that gives the trajectory a topographical definition amongst other "life lines" or social "world lines," and thus gives meaning to our lives.

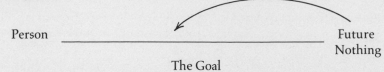

Person _____ Future
                                                  Nothing
                    The Goal

What we do is to seize one piece of the nothingness of our future and convert it into a quasi-concrete goal object lying on the trajectory of our life . . . we then live by this reified, hypostatized false end and, insofar as we live by it, we die of it. Any meaning derived from a source outside our acts murders us.   (Cooper, 1970, p. 87)

Lifton's outlook emphasized discontinuity; Cooper's highlights the subject's imaginative relation to the future. Both views say little about how the past is carried into the present. It is the latter point that we must understand if we are to grasp the relation between decision making and character development.

Richard Sennett realizes this and describes a view in which

the psychic reality of a life is not its momentary appearance but also its history.
    The essence of the possible adulthood I have described is that the individual would consciously accept, and feel comfortable with, the character of growth James and Freud depict. The guilt-based need of an ill person to wipe out the past and create a totally new self, at the same time that he is a slave to the past, is absent in this state of adulthood, for concomitant with an adult's ability to let new things in for themselves, to be free, is the capacity to accept earlier states of non-freedom as part of the sum total of who he is. This acceptance of the past's mosaic makes it something the individual need not continually relive in order to change it.   (Sennett, 1970, p. 123)

Sennett's last sentence hits close to the mark we have anticipated since we first noted the importance of the life-historical context of deciding. We clearly need a concept linking past and future, person and situation, objectivity and subjectivity. Such a dialectical notion is essential if we are to transcend the stale models currently on the market.

The person living

Our concern is to understand the *person living*, not the person's life. In the final systematic formulation of his philosophy, Jean-Paul Sartre (1960b) suggests a term designed to span both the life-structural and life-historical contexts of individual development, and, moreover, to force a perpetual return to the density of original experience: the *project*. The structure provided by this concept focuses attention on the specifics of how one is living, rather than on how one's life fits into general schemes.

A careful, but admittedly difficult, perusal of Sartre's definition of the project indicates why the notion is essential at this point of our inquiry:

> We affirm the specificity of the human act, which cuts across the social milieu while still holding on to its determinations, and which transforms the world on the basis of given conditions.
>
> For us man is characterized above all by his going beyond a situation, and by what he succeeds in making of what he has been made — even if he never recognizes himself in his objectification.
>
> The most rudimentary behavior must be determined both in relation to the real and present factors which condition it and in relation to a certain object, still to come, which it is trying to bring into being. This is what we call *the project*.   (Sartre, 1968, p. 91)

The term "project" in French and German has denotations which are useful to take into account in grasping Sartre's use of the word. It can mean a design, a sketch, a plan, an outline, a resolution. In verb form, to project means to throw forward with force, as a light on to a screen, a missile toward a target. When we speak of the project of a human subject, we lean on each of these meanings. We are concerned with the moving plan of the living person, a complex structure of intentions in relation to the objective world. An elaboration of a subject's project must therefore attend to the transcendence (*dépassement*) of situations as well as the ways in which the subject is determined by situations in the course of activity.

The project unfolds in a field of possibilities. The structure of that field depends on the social and historical reality in which the subject moves, even while the field is simultaneously constructed by the subject in response to needs and intentions. Sartre thus confirms our sense that in our attempts to understand the development of life structures, we cannot afford to ignore the system of objective and imaginary dependencies which underlie major decisions.

In Sartre's early biographical and philosophical studies, he proposes that the development of the project is determined by a "fundamental choice" made during youth, a private resolution to address the world in a characteristic style. So, for example, Genet adopts a label unfairly imposed on him by others and decides to be a thief. Baudelaire, in the wake of rejection by his beloved mother, chooses to live a solitary and miserable life.

We find ourselves again on the terrain of "character." Equipped this time around with an appreciation of character's role in life-structural transformations and with the notion of the project as guide, we can tackle several of the thorniest questions in the human sciences: in Chapter 8, the repetition compulsion and the nature of character development, and in Chapter 9, authenticity and sublimation.

Changing to stay the same

The study of decision making in relation to the contexts of life structure and life history confirms the falsehood of positive outlooks on character. Jacoby, in his extensive critique of neo-Freudian and post-Freudian humanistic psychologies, describes Theodor Adorno's position on character:

> Character, like personality, is a form of unfreedom. Against the neo-Freudians, who consider character a harmonious totality, Adorno interprets it as a result of a series of "shocks" inflicted on the individual; it bespeaks oppression and violence, not growth, choice, and values.   (Jacoby, 1975, p. 88)

This harsh view is corroborated by a leading psychoanalyst, Otto Kernberg. He depicts individuals in the *higher* levels of functioning as socially adapted, possessing stable self-concepts, and capable of guilt, mourning, and a wide variety of affect, *but* these same individuals are characterized by a severe, punitive superego, sadistic impulses leading to harsh perfectionism, inhibitory or phobic defenses, inhibited sexual drives, and Oedipal conflicts (Kernberg, 1977, Chapter 5).

In Chapter 1, the action of stereotypes was illustrated in Sherry's decision making. Now that our question concerns the extent to which decisions might affect character structure, the nature of stereotypes or interaction paradigms must be more fully understood.

Characteristic dispositions ("traits") develop as a consequence of repeated patterns of social interaction or traumatic events. These experiences form the core of the emotionally toned unconscious images of self-in-relation-to-others called stereotypes. An individual's emotional life gains its relatively restricted range from its linkage to this finite set of images.

Given the restricting structures of adult life, some dominant stereotypes are maintained in a state of total repression. Even a "well-defended" person may experience a vague self-estrangement, a feeling of not being oneself, particularly if intense meanings are attached to the stereotype. Suppressed yearnings find expression in inappropriate settings as a result. This is evident, for example, in a childless couple who scold or smother the neighbors' children, or when the responsible executive feels compelled to cut up boyishly in an important meeting. At a more serious level, the action inspired by stereotypes accounts for psychopathic murder, incest, suicide, kleptomania, and so forth.

These various types of "acting out" – actions carried out under the influence of unconscious fantasies and wishes (Abt and Weissman, 1976; Laplanche and Pontalis, 1973) – require either real or fantasized scenes in which to unfold. The coincidence of present situation and memory contribute to the sense of compulsion, urgency, and immediacy which always accompanies stereotypically informed acting out. Clinical studies demonstrate that acting out usually occurs when defenses are strained by fatigue, disappointment, or stress, with the direct aim of maintaining the repression of the painful memories associated with the stereotype. The connection to major life decisions can now be made.

Because decision points seem to offer a greater degree of openness than the routine of everyday life, because one is frequently stressed in the midst of dilemmas, because there is a zone of freedom ahead, suppressed impulses are particularly insistent and are likely to shape fantasies of what should be done to resolve dilemmas, just as dreams work through repressed wishes at night. A similar determination subtly moves the individual to construe situations along the lines of dominant characterological paradigms, to create the required scene. Anyone who has had the feeling that another is trying to pick an argument which would culminate in rejection or an angry fight is familiar with this slippery slide toward emotional catharsis.

In short, people may make significant alterations in life structures merely to avoid confrontations with themselves, to avoid the temporary breakdown of character structure which could, if properly resolved, result in a more autonomous mode of living.

Projected personal futures

The main evidence I can submit for this radical conclusion is derived from analyses of adult fantasies about prospects for the future. The drawing power of the future derives partly from its capacity to serve as an ambiguous blank screen for the projection of a reality blurred by stereotyped expectations. The process is like the prospector or archaeologist, pick-axe in hand, who "just knows" that *this time* of all times the gold or the lost city is only a few more swings away.

In the psychoanalytic view, a fantasy is "an imaginary scene in which the subject is a protagonist, representing the fulfillment of a wish (an unconscious one in the last analysis) in a distorted manner" (Laplanche and Pontalis, 1973, p. 314). A fantasy thus involves an imaginary projection of self into the future. To the degree that the wishes associated with core stereotypes achieve symbolic expression in a fantasied future, one finds it tantalizing. An aura hangs around its elements, making that image of the future glimmer and shine.

The most powerful fantasies are those which operate in a free zone, unrestricted by practical considerations. For this reason, I asked a number of interviewees to report fantasies of an ideal future. Sherry (from Chapter 1) turned out to have nourished one for some time. It clearly represents aspects of the core stereotypes we noticed earlier and creates a compromise with real factors that permits at least some gratification of lifelong yearnings. Other examples will be offered momentarily to illustrate the range of stereotypes which find their way into cherished images of future possibilities.

I'll give you my all-time fantasy, the best one I have. I am a musician and I'm going to end up marrying some dude that looks like a famous folk-rock singer and he's going to be a big person. He's going to have lots of money and be really famous, but every night when work is over, he's going to leave all that fame behind and he's going to become a nice human being daddy-type number. He's going to come home and we're going to have bunches of kids running around. All of our children are going to be musicians and our little girl will be a ballerina. And our boy will be a supermusician who can move his fingers on the guitar like Ravi Shankar on the sitar. They're both going to have really good voices. I'm going to have two more kids and they're going to have long dark hair and black eyes. . . .

I'll paint murals around my house. I'll have this big beautiful house but it's going to be like a cave with one exposed window. I'd have weird plants hanging around and a den with a lion and a couple of big dogs and cats. Everybody is going to get along very peacefully. Each room will have a different mood music. It's not going to be microwave-oven time either or McDonalds. Going to come home and have a nice dinner. The kids will have their own little talent show for the day and then when they go to bed, everything is gonna be nice and peaceful with a cozy fire and bearskin rug and the whole bit, you know. That's my fantasy.

This fantasy portrays a womb-like existence where nourishment is plentiful and Sherry is safe from harm. It also masks a wish for self-assertion that Sherry finds unacceptable, probably due to fears of transcending her mother's·condition. This wish is projected on to her husband, children, pets, artwork on the walls, and into the music which fills the air. Her glory comes from what goes on around her. She orchestrates the scene, doing nothing apparently. I asked her where she was in all of this. Her reply fortifies that she wants to feel significant through an ability to see her presence reflected back to her by her surroundings. This brings to mind the narcissism and the immanence of the traditional woman described by de Beauvoir in *The Second Sex* (1952).

Where are you in this fantasy?

I'm right in the middle.

What are you doing?

I'm being chief cook, bottle washer, and very talented person. I don't know. . . . I just dig on seeing things like that . . . wouldn't it be neat? Everybody have their own little goal, everybody talented.

You'd be a musician yourself in this fantasy?

Oh yeah, I would probably write all of my music just for my husband and he would go out and perform it for me, so together we would be making the money, but I could stay at home . . . his chief writer.

I also asked what her worst vision of the future would entail. Her reply allows us to nail down an interpretation of her more positive fantasies.

I'm gonna get laid off and never get called back and be on the ranks of welfare and have to go down and live in the inner city where all the muggings take place and my kids are gonna go barefoot and they're going to come in and take my kids away from me or something. That's the worst thing that could happen to me. To live in the slums, not have a job, not have any money . . . even to the point that my kids would be barefoot and halfway hungry, starvation. . . . As long as I can put food on the table and live here, I'm okay. I would be single, maybe become a harlot. . . . I had a dream about becoming a harlot one time. I woke up just as this dude was gonna beat me up for not doing it right or something. I woke up scared. One of the worst things that will probably happen to me, and it's quite possible, and it's really not so bad, is that I'll probably live with just me and my kids for a good number of years. . . . I don't foresee that as being really bad, but I do in a lot of ways.

A curious reappearance of the stereotype, particularly the feeling of being forced by circumstances into the dangerous position of the outsider, occurs here; simultaneously she stages a symbolic reversal of her anger toward men for putting her in this miserable condition and imagines being relieved of her dependent kids, the need to work, and of moral sanctions against open sexuality.

If we contrast the two fantasied futures, a dichotomy comes to light which takes us closer to a glimpse of the structure which would underlie Sherry's decisions about relationships with men. In the ideal version, she is not the outsider anymore. She is at the center of a protected place. There is food for all. The children are happy. (A "chief cook" must have food around; a "bottle-washer" is preparing to feed babies.) In the second fantasy, this scenario is reversed. She is not at the good center. She is out on the streets. She is hungry, perhaps childless. Her inclination toward dependency is so intense, she fears she might have to prostitute herself for companionship (just as she would go out in the cold with her grandfather to get the hot chocolate from her grandmother). Her current ambiguous situation, as Carl's mistress, is a compromise between the extremes of these dichotomies. He buys her groceries occasionally, but allows her some independence. She remains figuratively halfway between the slum-prostitute and the baby-mother in the cave-womb.

If the reader will recall the situation of Bill (Chapter 6), who had to join the Air Force Reserves for more money, but regretted it because he wanted to stay at home with his children, we can compare the effects of stereotypes and the degree to which they achieve expression.

I asked Bill what he would like to be if he had a chance to start all over again. He said that he had once considered being a pediatrician, but very quickly abandoned the idea. If he were to begin his education again, he might try that. Where would such an idea come from? In light of what we already know, it is not at all surprising. Bill enjoys being with children. He has financial problems. He would like to be like Jesus – taking care of sick children would approximate that role. Why didn't Bill go that route when he went to college? He gave me a fairly confused response to this question, but I gathered that he was referring to social-class factors. No one from his little working-class town had ever dreamed of actually trying to be a physician. It was bold enough of Bill to plan to be a computer scientist. Furthermore, that interest tied in with whatever masculine identifications he had been able to make with his mechanic father and grandfather. Taking care of kids was women's work. This is where the effects of stereotyped impulses become apparent. As we know, Bill's experiences with his mother were not likely to leave him with strong memories of warm and nurturant moments. His later discovery of these in his relationship with Susan was enough to clinch their marriage decision. For a person to sustain a nurturing role, and to make a career choice which requires a relatively continuous caring stance, a stronger characterological foundation would probably be necessary. This may be because images of another receiving what one has wished for oneself are difficult to tolerate. We saw how anxious Bill got when he was asking for more money and how much it bothers him to have his children wanting things from him that he cannot give. The decision not to be a pediatrician was probably reached immediately as these factors worked in conjunction with his sense of class position and academic ability.

If Bill's fantasy life were less restricted by anxieties of the sort we catalogued in Chapter 6, one would find that his actions came closer to finding compromises which permitted the expression of some of his lifelong yearnings. His temper tantrums would probably dissipate as well. One can imagine, for example, that some form of coaching work would allow him to satisfy a number of aims (being with children, involvement in sports, a socially approved zone for the expression of aggression). We discussed this possibility at one point, but Bill saw it as entirely impractical. In contrast to Bill, Sherry's character inclines her toward a dramatic enactment of her fantasies, despite attendant anxieties. Bill's concern for controlling impulses curtails the drama in his life and leaves him to live out a more conventional pattern.

I do not mean to imply that acting out fantasies is the key to successful decision making. The thrust of our previous conclusions leads one to realize that an ability to distinguish between stereotypically driven fantasies and more or less accurate representations of self-in-world would be ideal. Some would state the goals of psychoanalytic treatment in this manner – for example, Ferenczi:

> Certain characteristics common to those who have been thoroughly analyzed can . . . be mentioned. The far sharper severance between the world of fantasy and that of reality which is the result of analysis gives them an almost unlimited inner freedom and simultaneously a much surer grip in acting and making decisions; in other words, it gives them much more economic and more effective control.
> (Ferenczi, 1928, p. 211)

In some cases, stereotyped urges may be at work in a decision, even though it would be misleading to emphasize their influence. Other aspects of experience are frequently brought to light when one takes up a full life-historical perspective. For example, subcultural values, educational practices, normative behavior in peer groups, character training in sports, music, reading, religious activities, travel, and so on, contribute to decision processes in a preconscious manner, but are not necessarily dependent on the operation of repressed unconscious factors for their effect. Since the latter constrain decisions in a manner which is not generally acknowledged, they deserve special attention. Moreover, these unconscious factors seem to make the difference in determining the outcome of a decision.

Enigma variations

Freud wrote: "a thing which has not been understood inevitably reappears; like an unlaid ghost, it cannot rest until the mystery has been solved and the spell broken" (1909a, p. 122). And Sartre describes the unfolding of the project as having the same repetitive quality:

> The project never has any content, since its objectives are at once united with it and yet transcendent. But its coloration – i.e., subjectively, its taste; objectively, its style – is nothing but the surpassing of our original deviations. This surpassing is not an instantaneous movement, it is a long work. . . . For this reason a life develops in spirals; it passes again and again by the same points but at different levels of integration and complexity.
>
> (Sartre, 1968, p. 106)

Why do we often have the sense that we are repeatedly up against the same wall? Or that we have made a particular decision before?

In psychoanalytic literature, this phenomenon is known as the compulsion to repeat, and in grave cases, a "fate neurosis." In a classic case of the latter, a woman married three times, only to see each successive husband fall ill, requiring her to nurse them on their death beds (Freud, 1920).

We have seen what at least appears to be repetition in a number of cases, the only modification of the classic situation being that on occasion these respondents flip back and forth between the "winning" and "losing" positions in the repeated scenes.

Are these echoes of the past merely constructions we impose on a much more chaotic series of life events? Or, are the objective situations of life of such a limited variety that we necessarily pass through them repeatedly? These are both strong possibilities, yet they fail to account for our interviewees' "interest" in portraying their life histories in terms of repeated themes. Mary (Chapter 2) reduces her story to a quick "most of what I've gone through in my life is nothing but calling police, deciding whether or not to put abusive men in jail." She might have said, "nothing but trying to give my kids a pleasant childhood," or "nothing but trying to make ends meet" with equal veracity. I would argue that her primary unconscious self-representations and associated stereotypes motivate a sense of *real life* when she is in a threatened position. The drama, the action, the excitement, are located in those precarious moments. One must be careful not to assume that she therefore wants or desires or asks for abuse (as do several theories of masochism). It is more appropriate to view Mary as the victim of a character structure implanted in a society where male dominance, violence, and the objectification of women are glorified. We should not be surprised that her "cover story" carries headlines that tap into themes of general cultural interest. The repetition of painful situations, while privately suffered, deserves to be analyzed as a sociocultural problem.

Deliberation and character development

The notion of the life project challenges our usual ways of thinking about deliberation.

In the ordinary sense of the term, to deliberate is to hesitate in order to "think." The thinking one associates with deliberation is logical: it analyzes pros and cons, it seeks to construct feasible alternatives, and generally tries to approximate rationality of the sort proposed by cognitive psychologists. When the work of thinking is accomplished, a decision is likely to be at hand.

In this inquiry, we have seen that the life-historical embeddedness of an individual often reduces thinking to a means for rationalizing action guided by unconscious stereotypes. The thinking portion of deliberation is swept along on currents of emotion aroused by various powerful images of possible futures. Deliberation can thus serve as the bureaucratic functionary who puts the official seal on an organizational change which has already been effected. At most, deliberation manages to append a few conditional clauses or regulations to the new contract.

As soon as the authority of thinking as *the* prime mover of a decision is called into question, the process of making up one's mind can be seen for what it is. The language of deliberation provides some clues. It is a matter of "making up my mind." Doesn't this imply a degree of construction or fabrication, even falseness? Cosmetic "make up" covers blemishes and heightens attractive features. To "make up" an excuse, to "make up" a bed, to "make up" after a quarrel – all refer to the masking of something which cannot be accepted. Deliberation is about making something up because it attempts to cover over conflict in order to achieve a premature or haphazard unity.

Freud (1925) argued that thinking originated in the evolutionary process as a way of delaying action to avoid unnecessary risks. Actions are tested in imagination by recalling similar experiences, usually preconsciously, and responding in light of the effect associated with relevant experiences. Deliberation is thus predominantly a means of defining affective states to which we have access only through conscious ideation. Because affect can only be grasped through metaphorical expressions, the process of defining is always partial. Ambivalence stems from partial affective definition which leaves conflicting emotional responses to a possibility unresolved. Orthodox Freudian theory leads us astray in its failure to address critically social forms which for generations have needlessly engendered ambivalence-saturated personalities. From psychoanalytic literature one would get the impression that ambivalence is a personal problem. In Chapter 9, we examine the possibility of understanding it as the result of the way subjects internalize authority.

In anticipation of this point, consider Reich's (1945) claim that characterological ambivalence develops in the conflict between the individual's desire to lead a pleasurable and satisfying life and the real or imagined restrictions of the outer world. The first tendency of an individual is to be connected, involved, outgoing, and engaged with the world, but punishment, the loss of approval, and physical harm soon batter these life tendencies and create a foundation for ambivalence. Ambivalence is thus not an instinctual state, Reich argues, "it is a socially determined product of development" (1945, p. 274). Reich's character analyses show that decisional uncertainty generally follows from a fear of punishment and terror of the exercise of authority. The initial "splitting of the ego" which generates the unconscious realm is set up in this struggle between the demand of desire and the command of reality.

In readdressing the possibility that a decision might provoke character change, we can appreciate the potential for augmenting the autonomy of deliberation. If the power of unconscious stereotypes is due to their capacity to pull together motivation behind alluring images of future projects, and if indecision stems from a projection of past object-relational paradigms into expectations regarding the outcome of those projects, it would seem that a great deal of self-interpretive work could be carried out at decision points. The entire psychoanalytic enterprise would seem to recommend this. Fantasied futures can be analyzed in terms of the basic paradigms which underlie them, just as we speculatively examined the symbols of Sherry's imaginative self-projections. The constraints imposed by stereotyped impulses are not easily counteracted, but a process of interpretation, particularly a dialogical procedure in which those impulses can be directly experienced would contribute to their dismantling. Habermas (1968; cf. also Bleicher, 1980), propose the term "scenic understanding" for the manner of reflection which rationally reconstructs the relation of present intentions to prototypical scenes, convincing the subject of the futility of enacting a stereotyped drama yet another time. A Jamesian "heave of the will," drawing strength from the memory of repeated disappointment, would allow the subject to strike out on a tack more likely to be effective in achieving primary aims.

Kernberg (1977) conceives of character development in a different manner. The implications for decision making are parallel, however, to those just mentioned. Recalling the origin of stereotypes in the repression of negatively toned images of self-in-relation-to-others, development would entail a qualitatively new system of relations between self-image, object-image, and related affect. For this to occur, one would need to develop a tolerance for anxiety surrounding either images of separation of the self from an other, or for both good *and* bad qualities in self or other. A greater ability to see the self and the world realistically would follow from a differentiation of self from other, a capacity to experience contradictory emotions, and the subsequent clarity of perception. Decisions in which one's needs are grasped and acted on in a fashion less mediated by past misinterpretations gradually contribute to the construction of a foundation from which further progressive decisions may be made.

If such a view is not at least partially valid, "experience" would be of little use. The problem is to allow experience to be educative, and this is primarily a matter of life-historical self-interpretation. There is, however, no single way in which character structures change. Interpretation is clearly not the only way to bring it about. Occasionally, the accumulation of experience permits us to formulate spontaneous visions of what life *could* be and these images can impel progressive life changes.

THE JARGON OF AUTHENTICITY

Inauthenticity

> "The important thing is to understand what we are and to be it."
> (Ulo Betti)

The popular ethic which finds expression in such slogans as "Be true to yourself," "Express your inner nature," and "Get in touch with your feelings," are watered-down variants of a very serious philosophical proposition drawn from theology and passed down by existentialist philosophers. These statements are interpreted as encouragements to follow one's innermost feelings in choice and action. Beneath these slogans lies the assumption that humans are capable of and should strive for an *authentic* mode of living. This idea serves widely as a guide to conduct in secular circles, particularly for individuals who are searching for life meanings formerly afforded by spirituality.

A twentieth-century basis of the concern for authenticity is the German philosopher Heidegger's *Being and Time* (1927). In this work, Heidegger attempts to analyze the existence of the human individual in a manner which transcends the subject/object dichotomy paramount to western philosophy. Central to this intent is a redefinition of consciousness or the ego as *Dasein* ("being-there") which reflects Heidegger's assertion that there is no division between self and world:

Consciousness encompasses being. It is not "in here" but "out there."
The aspect of existence which makes this possible is human intentionality or concern.

The problem of authenticity arises as Heidegger investigates the
manner in which the individual is involved in the world. First, two
orders of being are distinguished. The first, the ontological, is purified,
detached from everyday concerns. The other, the "ontic," is practical,
common, and even "fallen." Intentions which are informed by the
latter are typically called "inauthentic" because they are subject to
public opinion, ordinary common sense, utility, and other stereotyped
modes of reasoning. On the basis of this distinction, inauthentic living
may be defined as a relating of self to the world in a way that denies the
real structure of the self or ignores real possibilities. The crowd, the
anonymous "they", is blamed for this failure of responsibility on the
part of the inauthentic individual:

> The Dasein becomes so involved in the necessary search for bread
> and in concern for what "they" say that he ignores above all the
> reality of his own existence.
>
> . . . the man who is caught up in the whirlpool of daily activity is
> the least straightforward in his dealing with things. Dasein gets so
> involved in "going along with the crowd" that soon he can no longer
> distinguish their catch words and pat formula answers from "what is
> revealed in pure understanding."   (Langan, 1961, pp. 22–6)

And what is characteristic of *authentic* modes of relation to being?
The response is abstract, yet it raises themes developed in our concrete
analyses of life structures and life projects.

> The authentic act of standing-in is an act of existence involving a
> self-extension toward what is unknown and *is* not yet, so that
> meaning may be brought to be and new explanation offered for the
> things that are. . . .
>
> Authentic existence, in fact, can only be something of an ideal, a
> direction to aim at amidst the dark reality of the dissimulation of
> everyday life.
>
> The authentic existent, who has discovered the miracle of his
> presence to the things-that-are, is ready to sacrifice all to the service
> of the creative renewing powers of his own poetic nature.
>
> (Langan, 1961, pp. 23, 25)

Heidegger assumes that we are inclined toward authenticity by our
capacity to experience a fundamental anxiety or anguish over our

finitude. The prototype of this anxiety may be found in the anticipation of death, an anxiety which could lead one to question everyday involvements.

> In the case of anguish . . . I begin to feel that I am losing my grip on the world. I begin to call into question the reality of my being and my place in the world. . . . It is in such a moment that I can suddenly come to realize that I am thrown into a world where I find myself among the things-that-are, that their presence before me depends on my opening a horizon of interpretation through the projection of comportment in relationship to them. . . .   (Langan, 1961, p. 37)

Heidegger encourages a struggle of a sort, not against the world, but against the tendency in oneself to keep the world out. He, along with his current spokesman, Gadamer, seeks a peaceful "dwelling" in the midst of being. Langan's commentary puts it a bit too vigorously to be faithful to the original:

> The limitations of past existence make themselves felt on every level of the individual's life, from the limitations of a tradition down to the limitations deep within the structure of the life that I have built for myself amidst the cries and hues of daily existence. In the future I must pay the "debt" of limitations inherited from the past, in the sense that I must be determined to struggle beyond the more crippling limitations. This is in part what Heidegger means by resolution. . . . Resoluteness is constant fight in the face of a world formed by the inauthentic existence of others and against the burdens of our own condition which tend always to pull us back toward authenticity. . . . Resolution opens up a field for the authentic exercise of freedom, for in projecting on the basis of my essential situation I am freed from the meaningless domination of the anonymous "they."   (Langan, 1961, pp. 37-3)

Adorno's critique

Heidegger's outlook would seem to fit perfectly our need for a description of how an individual becomes subjected to the social order. But is it simply a matter of not taking responsibility for one's actions or concerns? The general existentialist understanding is that we allow others, the "they," to take responsibility. And since "they" is no one in particular, everyone gets off the hook. This is an apt characterization of a common attitude, yet there is a serious oversight in Heidegger's analysis. The anonymity of the "they" is a function of the individual's acceptance of what "they" do and say. No one bothers to wonder who exactly says or does it and why. What Heidegger's analysis occludes is that, in any case we choose to specify, "they" is actually someone in particular, or some aggregate (although perhaps not a formal organiz- ation) whose interests are served by the perpetuation of what "they" say.

The domination of *Dasein* by the "they" is said to be sustained partly by "idle talk" or "chatter." This idea is challenged by the German philosopher and culture critic, Theodor Adorno, in *Negative Dialectics* (1966) and *The Jargon of Authenticity* (1973), a devastating critique of Heidegger's entire system.

The key to Adorno's critique is the recognition that certain modes of discourse have the function of rationalizing and masking "harsh realities." Heidegger's existentialism has a lulling quality. Its language is vague and strangely cozy. For anyone who has been swept away by Heidegger's jargon, passages like the following from Adorno are startling:

> Heidegger imposes the critical diagnosis of a negative ontological status on the "everyday being of the *Da*, existence," which in truth is historical in nature: the entangling of the mind with the sphere of circulation . . . as if by a fungus which stifles the quality of thought. This confusion has arisen and can be gotten rid of; we do not need to bemoan it and leave it in peace as if it were the essence of *Dasein*. . . . Chatter would already be in decline if, in a reasonable economy, the expenditure of advertisements disappeared. Chatter is forced on men by a social structure which negates them as subjects long before this is done by newspaper companies. . . . [Heidegger] condemns idle chatter, but not brutality, the alliance with which is the true guilt of chatter, which is itself far more innocent.
>
> (Adorno, 1973, pp. 101–2)

Adorno reminds us that language is mediated by the objective world to which it refers. Heidegger has cut us off from the possibility of realizing this by his division of being into the purified (ontological) and the fallen (ontic) realms. The interests of everyday life, be they economic, political, agricultural, or educational, are relegated to the state of inauthenticity. Concern for such things is not where meaning resides for the academic philosopher. The authentic life moves in the world of language, poetry, ideas. In glorifying that "higher" world, Heidegger reinforces the hand of those whose decisions co-ordinate the practical world and administer the public opinion which comes to be a part of the "they."

At one point in *Being and Time*, Heidegger vigorously asserts that *Dasein* (human existence) "is in each case mine," it owns itself. This seems to imply that we cannot forget the individuality or uniqueness of a particular subject, that no one else shares the same existence. Simultaneously, a certain responsibility is suggested: If Dasein is mine, I am responsible. At first glance, the possibility of authenticity would seem to rely on this capacity to "own" one's intentions and to make decisions in that context, but there is a difficulty with this terminology. For Heidegger, owning oneself is only authentically possible in the ontological realm, beyond everyday concerns. In a very important passage, Adorno counters:

> The jargon cures Dasein from the wound of meaninglessness and summons salvation from the world of ideas into Dasein. Heidegger lays this down once and for all in the title deed, which declares that the person owns himself. . . . The distinction between authenticity and inauthenticity — the real Kierkegaardian one — depends on whether or not this element of being, Dasein, chooses itself, its mineness. Until further notice, authenticity and inauthenticity have as their criterion the decision in which the individual subject chooses itself as its own possession. The subject, the concept of which was once created in contrast to reification, thus becomes reified. . . . By the fact that it is ontological, the alternative of authenticity and inauthenticity directs itself according to whether someone decides for himself or not. It takes its directive, beyond real states of affairs, from the highly formal sense of belonging to oneself. Yet its consequences in reality are extremely grave. Once such an ontology of what is most ontic has been achieved, philosophy no longer has to bother about the societal and natural-historical origin of this title deed, which declares that the individual owns himself. Such a philosophy need no longer be concerned with how far society and psychology allow a man to be himself or become himself. . . . *The societal relation, which seals itself off in the identity of the subject, is de-societalized into an in-itself. The individual, who himself can no longer rely on any firm possession, holds on to himself in his extreme abstractness as the last, the supposedly unlosable possession.*   (Adorno, 1973, pp. 114–15, my emphasis)

In short, authenticity has little to do with distancing oneself from practical concerns in the everyday world. There is no uncontaminated way of life beyond the machinations of society. Heidegger's philosophy, and existential psychology in general, may be interpreted as a final assertion of "individuality" or "subjectivity" in the face of a set of social relations which has rendered these concepts suspect (Jacoby, 1975). In other words, only the person for whom individuality or authenticity is problematic needs to claim these characteristics so hysterically. Adorno locates the problem not in Heidegger's realms of being, but in the contradictions of social relations.

And what of Heidegger's claim that the experience which leads one to break from the "they" in order to become authentically oneself is anxiety? Anxiety has a special meaning for Heidegger, but whatever the form anxiety takes, we know that it generally inclines one either toward conformity or toward automatic impulsive behavior of a stereotyped nature. The central flaw in Heidegger's analysis is his failure to acknowledge that self-interpretations are constrained, that my grasp of what I essentially am is likely to be stereotyped, just as any idea I have contains elements of the "idle talk" of public opinion. We saw in Chapter 8 that projections and decisions made on the basis of my "essential situation," particularly those in which I feel most like myself, most at one with who I am, are clearly grounded in the more intensely conflicted interaction paradigms or stereotypes.

Another side of authenticity is defined by one's relation to temporality – to the past, present, and future. Projections into the future can only be made on the basis of what is and has been. Heidegger's language suggests that a positive relation to the past is essential for authenticity: "My dwelling in the things-that-are requires that I actively let the objective thing be" through my own discourse. Adorno claims that this outlook preserves the identity of the subject to himself or herself. One merely *becomes* what one *was*.

In a number of interviews conducted in my study of decision making, people were struggling with issues closely linked to those we have been treating abstractly above. One individual in particular forced me to clarify my thinking about the notion of authenticity – about what it might mean to decide authentically. As Adorno suggested, the issue revolves around the preservation or contradiction of personal *identity*.

The self as other

Nathan, 36, whose general life story we pondered earlier, responded to my ad requesting interviews with people who were in the midst of making an important decision. He was thinking of quitting his job as a legal aide and was unsure about what to do next. This was not the first time he had contemplated a career change. He had gone through the process at least five times already.

When we met for the first interview, I explained my project briefly and he began to speak, in a careful and deliberate manner:

> I have willed to do a lot of things and I have made a lot of decisions. I have accepted responsibility for them. I used to believe that I just drifted from one thing to another, but it's clear that at a point, I decided to plan, to control rationally. I had a sense of taking control of myself.

Nathan is referring to the point when, at 17, he ran away from home. He portrays his father as a tyrant who took pleasure in frightening his children into obedience. Two examples symbolize the ongoing terror. To keep the children from coming downstairs to play, the father once hung butcher knives on strings above the stairway. At another point he left a live electrical wire exposed in the bathroom for weeks, and menacingly told the children not to touch it if they wanted to stay alive. Nathan also reports being forbidden to read, study, or do anything which might indicate an intent to transcend his father's rough working-man mentality.

For our purposes, we need not understand the reasons behind the behavior of Nathan's father. It is sufficient to know that an authoritarian and sadistic style prevailed, especially as Nathan remembers it.

After leaving home, Nathan got into a number of painful situations and is puzzled now by the length of time it took him to get out of them. One such situation was a teaching position. He felt he had a good relationship with the students, but little support from the administration. He kept wallowing in feelings of dissatisfaction and even toyed with the idea of quitting, but was unable to articulate his frustration.

> Then one day I was attacked at school. A student pinned me against a wall with a desk. It wasn't directed at me, I was just the object of aggression. I was in the way. I looked at him and decided to quit teaching. I told the principal I wanted to leave. It was hard to detach, but I was a stranger. I did not belong there, so I left. I felt squeezed.

I suggest that this scene recapitulates scenes that forced Nathan to leave home. He felt a stranger there. He felt like a mere object, a target for aggression. He reports sensing that there was nothing wrong with him in particular; he was just in his father's way. His father "didn't *mean* what he was doing." Since those scary days at home, a feeling of being in jeopardy often pervades Nathan's experience. What sort of jeopardy? Jeopardy of being "pinned," objectified, reduced, being cut off, being insignificant. Whatever the form the feeling takes, and we will inquire into several of these, this vulnerability is not only experienced in relation to the father. The oppressive aspects of all social life stand out for Nathan. He has been threatened by real violence and his fear of being violated further spreads to a number of situations, making it quite difficult for him to experience any satisfaction in his achievements, or in his productivity.

As an example of this point, consider Nathan's experience with weaving. A friend had shown him how to do weaving on a primitive loom. Nathan built his own, completed a large section of cloth, and cut it off the loom. He fell into a deep depression which lasted three days. A woman happened to visit and told Nathan he could sell the cloth at a certain store. When he took the cloth there, a customer saw it, wrapped it around herself, and bought it. Nathan again had the "horrible feeling" he had experienced when he cut the cloth from the loom: "Now, every time I finish weaving cloth, I feel a dread. I feel like I'm attacking myself when I cut it off. I fear that it will be attacked. There is a sense of exposing myself, a sense of jeopardy. I don't want to think that I am vulnerable."

I began to wonder what weaving might mean to Nathan. He says his interest in it came out of the blue. Since people do not believe that he taught himself, he tells them that his grandmother told him how. He is bothered by this untruth, but no one believes him when he tells the truth. Part of the truth is that weaving has to do with the past: perhaps not with his grandmother, but at least with earlier figures in his life. As he explained:

> Weaving is an *ancient* thing. I don't care for the cloth. I care for the process. I take fleece from an animal and spin it into string and make something that can be practical or decorative. I handle every aspect of the process myself. That is significant. It signifies me.

How could the act of weaving possibly "signify" Nathan? It would not be stretching things too much to see in this a hope of moving symbolically through his own socialization experience, taking control of it this time, deciding for himself when it should be cut off. This process of movement from nature through an intermediate stage to a culmination in an artistic or utilitarian product definitely parallels the process of "sublimation," in which socially unacceptable drives are translated into desired activities. In this case, it is a move from *chaotic* fleece to *orderly* cloth, an order which bears the organization Nathan imposes on it. His own subjective activity is objectified in the cloth. Alienation is overcome *in the process of weaving*. But, when he cuts the cloth off, when it becomes a commodity for others to do with what they want, the transcendent state breaks down. Nathan is reduced to a role when the process is over. He becomes *a weaver*, not the one who does the weaving. He fights this feeling vigorously.

What would be sufficient for Nathan? Why is it difficult for him to find an activity which continues to be satisfying and builds naturally on itself, rather than having to be cut off? Since he seemed to be in a position to inform me about problems of authenticity in decision making, I pursued the topic, focusing on the pattern of recentering which had characterized his life to that point. Nathan admitted being quite puzzled by that pattern. He studied piano for twelve years and dropped it. He took photographs and collected a gallery-full of negatives, but never had them printed. He studied general subjects for years to become a teacher. After five years he quit. These "fits and starts have been successful for the most part," he said, "but they don't have any extension . . . I've made the decision about clipping them. I cut them off. I guess I don't understand why I do that with my experience in the world." His exaggerated claim to responsibility made me inquire about his manner of "owning" these choices.

When I do something I do it authentically or I don't do it. When I discover that I'm not, I stop.

What do you mean by authentic?

Why are you confused? It's simple. If it is authentic, then it is *meant*. It is appropriated and it is thorough. You have appropriated the past thoroughly. You explore it, you pick it up, and you know it.

Appropriated?

In my relationship with someone, I *mean* to be in a relationship with that person, not with a projection of my needs. On the basis of the real nature of our interaction, I can say, after a period of time, "I *unconditionally* want a relationship with who you are, until I discover something that is so threatening to my integrity that I can no longer say that the relationship is unconditional."

He described teaching in a similar vein, tacking on the same escape clause: "I unconditionally and authentically was a teacher until I discovered that there was something about that process that was insufficient for me as a *living being*. I needed another arena. I identified that need in myself and had to change."

Recalling the event that triggered Nathan's decision to quit teaching and his experience with his father, we see that the threat to integrity associated with leaving situations has often been a threat to his *bodily* integrity. The "split self" which Nathan tries to avoid has some basis in a fear of bodily harm, even of disintegration and of no longer being a "living being."

Here, a brief interlude of contemporary French psychoanalysis will be useful.

The premier psychoanalyst of the 1960s and 1970s in Paris was Jacques Lacan. He proposes (LeMaire, 1977) that for an individual to come to have a sense of being a subject, a unified "I," it is necessary to pass through a "mirror phase" in which the relatively fragmented experience of the body is gradually replaced by a wholeness and connectedness under the "I." The emergence of the subject into language is set up, although not achieved, by this identification which covers over the gap between self and other. The events which bring about this "accession to language" need not involve real mirrors. It is for an other that one becomes constituted as a subject. For example, one speaks to the other in order to express desire.

Lacan (1966) also proposes that the child's movement into the symbolic order of culture and language is precipitated by the threat of castration, of being cut off, cut up, and kept apart from what it takes to survive. The experience of self-as-subject depends on this embeddedness in the cultural reality: "The symbolic order is constitutive for the subject." The mirror phase assures that one is concerned for the self from the point of view of an other; the law of the father (authority, police, castration, the "they") fixes the subject in a subjected position.

I suggest that Nathan is attempting to master issues directly related to this early stage of development. His concern is with the violence surrounding the way in which he becomes an object for others. The synthesis he sets up between subject and object in the process of deciding is not adequately capturing the desire which he seeks to express. The core of the problem is that this desire, as Lacan would put it, is "alienated in the other." Where Nathan feels alive in the process of teaching, being a lover, or weaving, the other in himself looks at the objective aspect of the process – the teacher, Nathan's body, the cloth.

Weaving is a surprise for me, because I found myself expressing myself in a way I thought I never would. I thought I was filling up some spare hours, doing something to break up the monotony. But what I found was that I made something that meant something to somebody else. When I looked at what I did, I didn't feel anything! When I look at myself in the mirror, I don't feel anything! It's difficult. It's difficult. Other people saw something there.

So Nathan produces an object that gains the recognition of the other. They want what he produces. He does not want it himself. His life activity is reduced to an object for exchange. But only a particular aspect of the process bothers him consciously:

> What I reacted to was the completion of the task, not the object I had made. It was the process that was the problem with me. That was the issue.

What are you trying to work out?

> I'm not sure. Take the example of drawing. I started drawing. I felt the same thing. Then I stopped drawing. I had submitted a portfolio to an art school, but as soon as I got accepted I stopped drawing. Drawing is a very painful thing for me to do. It's physically painful. Just one line can make an incredible difference in the whole drawing. As I made a line, I could *feel* its impact on me rather than on the paper. Anyway I stopped.

The pattern is certainly there. What is it? It seems like it's usually a sudden thing.

> It's filled with jeopardy.

Note that as a legal aide Nathan would be familiar with the legal use of the term "jeopardy" – hazard of being found guilty – but guilty of what? My inclination is to see it as guilt about not really being what he pretends to be, of not accepting the distinguishing "line" he draws in his activities, of intentionally misleading others in order not to be pinned down. But this contradicts his yearning to be recognized by others for what he actually is rather than as an object, a role, or a mere producer.

> In Boston, this man *saw me*. I walked into his gallery. He looked at my weavings, he priced them at $1000 apiece. He was dealing with *me*. When I got back here, I had vanished from view. No one here treated me with that regard or awareness. He *knew* me. He understood me. It hasn't occurred since then, and that was four years ago.

I wondered why, if Nathan had at last felt recognized as a weaver, he was not pursuing it still. Was it that he was being recognized as something he did not want to be? To some extent, yes. He admits not liking fiber arts. He prefers drawing, painting, film, and writing. They involve more challenging ideas, he says. So perhaps he can only do well, and complete, projects he is not invested in.

> Well, see, what I don't want to do is anything other than what I'm supposed to do, than what I really want to do. I may not even have

the courage to name what I really want to do. So . . . you're good to get me to say this . . . this is terrible [laughs] . . . I don't know what I want to do yet.

Which will it be: what he is supposed to do, or what he really wants to do? I asked him, after he admitted not wanting to say something and not having the courage to *name* what he really wants to do, what exactly he was not wanting to name. He recounted his history in more detail this time:

I can say that rather than just thinking about various occupations I have acted them out. I've been a foreman in a factory. I've worked on a ship. I've been a steward at a port. I've been a teacher. I've worked in a law office and in a brokerage house. I've not trusted just thinking what something might be like . . . I've tried it. On the one hand, it was out of curiosity and at another level, it was acting out, trying to get these encounters out of my system. So what have I put myself through this for? Part of it has been learning to be alone and coming to see that I am an individual through playing lots of different kinds of roles, to see that standing behind the roles is a person. So what I've had to come to grips with is my own person.

Which is?

Lots of perceptions, judgments, ideas, feelings that I can name, that I can identify as my own. Now that I have some sense of my self, maybe I'm trying to decide "What will I do with me?" Given what I think about my world, my culture, my relationships with other individuals, what do I do with all this?

So in terms of your original question, my decision is: How do I wish to proceed? How do I see myself as best being a contributing member of this society and this community? What can I do that might help?

In Nathan's attempts to recenter on activities he authentically intends, we see a form of constantly calling himself into question as if he works under the eye of a very strict supervisor. He acts as if no accomplishment, no identity, could possibly pass the supervisor's test. It is not a matter of quality, however. Nathan knows that what he does is done very well. Is it a problem of coming to terms with endings? Of fearing that nothing will end well and so ending things before the feared ending occurs on its own? It seems more probable, given the evidence presented to this point, that Nathan is afraid of becoming a "subject" in the gaze of the other. Recognition would unmask him, forcing him to see himself as others see him. This would not be traumatic except for the lesson he learned early on from his father: that to be a subject, for example, to achieve or stand out, was to set himself up as an object for his father's abuse. How is this related to the multiple career changes Nathan has initiated? How does this inform us about the jargon of authenticity?

In our final interview, I raised these questions again. I first asked him to tell me more about the pattern of recentering that characterized the course of his life. He immediately related those frequent changes to the feeling of jeopardy which preceded them. He covered over this memory of feared and/or experienced violence with a claim that the various experiences were no longer interesting: "I don't like to wear experiences thin. When I find that everything is going to become chatter, when the routine seems to lose its significance, when it has become grey, I don't want anything to do with that." My conclusion that he defends against the jeopardy of violence/castration is reinforced by his next statement. The lack of authentic relation to the activity *follows* the sense of jeopardy.

Below he refers to an interest in linguistics that was then developing. Note that he anticipates the jeopardy, not the sense of estrangement, alienation, or inauthenticity.

> If I see something emerging, that is exciting. It is provocative. It is something that I discover in myself, like my new interest in language and culture. It is a real thing. It's something making a connection between out there and inside. There is a lot of self-doubt still, but I'll be damned if I'll let myself be overrun, overwhelmed.

Nathan then brought up his decision to quit teaching. This time he failed to mention the attack in the classroom. It was merely a matter of "not growing" and of the activity being "insufficient." To grow or to make an activity sufficient hardly necessitates leaving it. We are still unable to understand the need to recenter, to shift to an entirely new field. In the process of trying to comprehend this a peculiar thing happened in the interview. As I tried to pin Nathan down, he kept slipping away into another topic or example. Occasionally he would attempt to turn the table on me by making me the subject of interrogation. It was clear that he felt in jeopardy. I was getting close to making him confront a painful realization that he had masked for years in the jargon of authenticity. He went into his refrain:

> I am not a teacher; I'm a person who teaches. I am not a linguist; I am a person who can understand linguistics. In my relationship with

one person, I'm bringing my self to it, all of me. I have a history that I carry along with me. I'm not just a person who is sitting here now. I'm bringing my whole history forward. . . . What I have chosen to do has changed. I haven't disappeared and reappeared periodically as one thing or another. I'm always around. I may choose to go elsewhere, but that doesn't mean I have disappeared! I'm just in another place.

I began to wonder if I would have formed an entirely different picture of Nathan if I had been studying the nature of self-esteem, or another continuous process, rather than decisions. In response to a question along those lines he said the picture would probably not be different. I refocused my question one last time:

The thing I'm interested in here is that you have changed roles many, many times, to the extent that you recognize a pattern in the way you do this. What is the relation of that to your history?

Oh ho ho. That is an enormous question. It would take years to answer that. It would be difficult to capture. But the main consistency in the pattern is virtue. I can remember the first big problem I had with myself as a person was that I had lied and I recognized it as a lie. It just destroyed me. That is constant.

Not wanting anything to be a lie?

Not wanting anything to be wrong or evil or wicked or nasty.

This is important, because I was getting the sense that, in a certain way, there is a will to trick other people.

Oh, no, that's not true.

Let me tell you where that idea comes from. You have said, "Here's something I enjoy, but I'm not there. Here's something else I like, but I'm not there either. I'm just the person who was doing that." It's like you're saying "I'm over here! Ha, ha, no I'm not! Now I'm over here! Catch me if you can!" But what you say you're doing is just the opposite of that. You're saying that for you to stay where you were, or where I have seen you would be a lie to yourself.

Right. And it is the responsibility of the other to come to terms with who I am.

The Other wants you to stay the same. They want to know whom they are addressing.

But they *do* know! There's a tremendous problem with seeming and being in our culture. It has to do with masks. I'm trying not to wear one. Well, we all wear something like a mask. We all have a role. I just want my mask, my role, to encompass who I am. There are limitations to any role, but I want to be that role authentically. I want the role to correspond to who I am.

Any commitment, though, reduces the whole potential self to a partial actual self. Any decision to undertake a project generates activity that is partial, a compromise between doing nothing and being perfect. The guilt Nathan labors under, the sense of jeopardy that builds up over time as necessary lies must be told to others and to oneself, make virtuosity nearly impossible. Nathan's decisions to abandon activities seem to be ways of leaving those histories behind, probably to avoid the oppressive sense of guilt over possible achievements, however much he claims to carry his history forward with him. Each decision to cut off a project restores him to guiltless anonymity but short circuits accomplishments which might bring on the internalized father's disapproval or self-condemnation for imperfection. The jargon of authenticity thus masks the violence which lurks both in homes and in the social relations of the marketplace. The woman who wrapped herself in Nathan's cloth without recognizing its maker commits a minor act of violence. Even the man who *knew* Nathan as the artist had to pin price tags on what for Nathan was primarily of emotional value. The strategy Nathan adopts to cope with these pressures backfires. Self-objectification is essential to the accomplishment of projects. In order to avoid objectification by others, Nathan blocks the movement of his own subjectivity, becoming stagnant and ineffective with regard to the world.

Nathan's account demonstrates that "authenticity" is a misleading image of effective being-in-the-world, contrary to what Heidegger suggests. The attitude of authenticity reflects a state of mind which preserves the identity of the subject to himself. In other words, the jargon of authenticity is recruited when the subject feels threatened, or is forced by objective circumstances to become other than what it has been. The individual's concept of self – as a certain sort of person, behaving in specific ways – would have to change. Such change, given the linkage of self-representations to key object-relational paradigms, is actually painful. Hence, the interpersonal showdowns which characterize relationships these days often end up in a stalemate, both parties asserting their need to be "who they are," unwilling to conceive of ways to redefine their existence in mutually satisfying terms: "I am just this way and you will have to accept me as I am." The cult of authenticity gets things twisted around. The authentic subject denies his determination and projects it into the future: "I will be who I am." The inauthentic becomes anything which is not identical to itself. This freezes the dialectic of the life project Sartre described. Adorno reminds us that when speaking of the human subject, we must consider both the notness of what one is (the ways in which we are limited by social conditions from achieving a humane way of life, for example) and the somethingness of what one is not (the real possibilities, given actual states of social development, which might be open to individuals and groups if only they were able to recognize their situation). The subject which strives to be what it is, Adorno concludes, becomes nothing but itself. And, as we have seen repeatedly, the subject is typically lured into believing that what it is is its own creation, a natural outcome of processes that had to be accepted if not ignored.

The jargon of authenticity has a few cousins we noted earlier. Mary spoke of seeking "justice" when she was actually planning to strike back harder than she had been hit. Bill's concern for "caring" and "kindness" masked an inner turmoil that threatened to bubble over. Sherry's jargon of "autonomy" and "independence" concealed her anger over humiliating rejection and her struggle with loneliness. Beyond the general tendency for rationalization to look on the bright side of life, we see that it can actually prevent a confrontation with the truth of one's history and situation. To the extent that this is the case, major decisions are made in a falsified world, in accordance with ideas that mask oppressive features of social life and perpetuate a dialectic of domination and reactive aggression.

Negativity for a change

Nathan's battles against the "identity" culture reflect the possibility of an authenticity not subject to Adorno's criticism. This would involve meaning what one does and knowing what one means. Simultaneously, statements of personal identity – "Now and forever, I am so" – would have to be resisted.

If this outlook is at all feasible, the laudatory press for acts of *sublimation* will need to be called into question. Sublimation is the process whereby the insistence toward expression of stereotyped impulses is displaced into activities which are harmless and culturally acceptable, or even better, into culturally valued creative work. Recent French psychoanalytic thought challenges this standard understanding of the term: sublimation is merely the process by which the action suggested by an impulse is constrained and its investment is displaced into a symbolic representation (Silvestre, 1979, p. 25). The true object of the stereotyped action – a sexual or aggressive aim, in the typical case – is abandoned, to the profit of the symbolic order in which the subject is embedded. This substitution process "is a circuit, forever repeated, and even if enjoyment is expected, it is at best only a means for the subject to count the circuits as each is accomplished" (p. 13). Sublimation is thus a means of avoiding the real, a "derivative means by which the speaking being is able to let himself speak – perhaps in the most common form of chatter . . ." (p. 24).

If sublimation is such a waste of time, and acting out stereotyped impulses directly is neurotic, unfree, and usually impossible due to social prohibitions, what alternative remains?

Aware of the potential stalemate, Shiff writes:

> Life as art allows neither change nor growth; art as life conveys no meaning. Our world lies between the two extremes. In effect we shift back and forth along the metaphoric bridge; our life is modeled on our art, and our art is modeled on our life. In this way we maintain ourselves as individuals in a state of doubt.
>
> (Shiff, 1978, p. 120)

That recurring word "doubt," implying continual self-questioning, must hold the key to the demetaphorized action we seek. Not acting out, not posing, not acting "as if" – merely aiming to do that which one reflectively chooses to be engaged in.

Realizing that major decisions involve the co-ordination of many inner voices, this demetaphorizing doubting would inquire, "Who is speaking?" "What intentions are to be fulfilled?" "Who am I addressing?" The fuller the narrative of self-questioning becomes, the weaker the need to *decide*. The action that will prove to be most effective appears in the clearing created as the confusion is interrogated away. This attitude of *negativity* could counteract the power of unconscious representations of self-in-relation-to-others, rendering compelling impulsive projects merely tentative, and empowering autonomous reasoning.

T·E·N

FRAGMENTS ON IDEOLOGY

> He pictures himself as the individualist who whistles at the world. But what he whistles is its melody.   (T. W. Adorno, 1938, p. 293)

Taking into account only the limited set of life narratives we have studied, one finds an amazingly long list of social problems confronted in these modern decisions: spouse abuse, poverty, isolation, welfare living, divorce, unemployment, lack of community, aimlessness, exhaustion in meeting role requirements, war, unwanted pregnancy, fear on the streets, and so on. These problems could be understood separately, but the perspective we gain through a critical analysis of decision making enables us to specify a general condition which characterizes the majority of dilemmas: *the subjection of consciousness to relations of power, force, and authority.*

This implies much more than the idea that we tend to follow laws and make choices in accordance with social norms. Obviously many people do not. The point is that the psychological force of the social context operates very subtly, yet ubiquitously. The social structures and historical processes which influence us, as if from behind our backs, *appear* to be working safely at a distance, unrelated to the immediate problems of everyday life such as those faced by the participants in my research. A closer look at the social underpinnings of the deciding consciousness reveals that social macrostructures are integral to the genesis and structure of the psyche itself.

This is hardly a new idea. Yet, psychologists and citizens alike tend not to grasp the implications for social practice that follow from this notion. A few quick forays into psychopathology, philosophy, and contemporary social theory will provide a solid basis for understanding these implications: first, the concept of the sadomasochistic structure of narcissism; second, the master-slave dialectic; and, finally, the critical notion of ideology.

Sadomasochism

A strange implication of our analysis is that people who have problems making decisions may be fortunate. The fact that their decisions are problematized reveals a sensitivity to contradictions in the social order. To be without decision problems may indicate a failure to be affected by the issues of one's epoch. The non-decider becomes the exploited tool of larger processes which he or she affirms primarily because the *status quo* seems omnipotent and necessary.

Even those for whom decisions are radically problematized are nevertheless subject to the eradication of autonomy by ideological processes. An ideological process involves the captivity of consciousness by images, feelings, and impulses that channel one's action toward submissive or merely reactive modes. These actions can be interpreted as ideological when they serve to bolster existing social structures that perpetuate domination. The link between personal choices and social processes is difficult to establish, but if one searches for an answer to the question, "Why are people willing to put up with their subjection and misery?", the intricacies of major life choices become a prime arena for suspicion. In our private choices, the oppressive order of the external world finds expression.

In Chapter 9, we saw how individuals can make sudden changes in significant life spheres primarily as a way of doing something to themselves that had been done to them. We have also noticed that important choices are made in a flinging, jumping, snapping, or flipping action of the psyche. Something seems to snap into place and resists dismantling. It becomes too late to change one's mind or to turn back. These are feelings, not realities. Most of these choices could actually be reversed.

It is not sufficient to explain this locking movement as the result of an unconscious stereotyped impulse, as a "return of the repressed." Here, we are confronted with a specific stereotype that reflects a particular experience in social interaction. Consider the possibility that we make drastic decisions out of anxiety that has its roots in relations of domination. The hesitating individual, fearful of failure, punishment, disapproval, or ostracism, leaps towards life patterns in which it is possible to recognize his/her appropriate place. The demands of "conscience," "reality," and "desire" fuse into a compromise that appears as the "only way to go." This foreclosure of possibilities and the associated rush into one's proper place is the hallmark of ideology.

There is an aggressive moment in this coerced compromise. As the identification necessary to seal the decision develops, significant wishes are *cut off*. A punishment is meted out against the self or the Other as anxiety-provoking forbidden impulses begin to emerge in fantasied futures. This punishment, this violence against desire, becomes a part of the momentum that makes modern choices possible despite the incredible complexity of modernity.

The psychodynamic basis of this odd reaction is best described as a *sadomasochistic* phenomenon. The syndromes of sadism and masochism have suffered from wide and careless usage, and a debate still rages in psychoanalytic literature to determine what sorts of psychopathology, if any, deserve to be understood under these rubrics. For our purposes, it will most useful to define sadomasochism as a defensive maneuver designed to strengthen an ego threatened by fragmentation. This maneuver is likely to be necessary when a negatively toned object-relational stereotype is elicited by the thematic resemblance of a current life situation to an emotionally conflicted scene from the person's past life. The sadomasochistic defense takes either the self or an other as an object to be deprived, hurt, or otherwise punished. In so doing, the energies bound to the repressed stereotype find a channel for expression without forcing a reorganization of personal identity.

Recent psychoanalytic analyses (for example Gear, Hill, and Liendo, 1981) show that a sadomasochistic structure underlies the personality disorder known as narcissism. This is particularly significant, for contemporary sociocultural analyses of American life provide evidence that aspects of narcissism permeate the culture of advanced industrial society (cf. Lasch, 1979; Kovel, 1981). At the core of narcissism is an intense childhood rage toward socializing agents. This rage can probably be traced to the alternating over- and under-gratification typical of modern childrearing in affluent families, and to physical punishment in general. Since the expression of anger on the child's part is not tolerated and is severely punished, the child develops a debilitating guilt for harboring hostile feelings and simultaneously internalizes images of violent others into his/her self-concept. To compensate for the resultant low self-esteem and self-deprecation, an ever vigilant eye attends to the reactions of others. Approval is sought at every turn. Others are manipulated to grant positive attention. The image of self in the regard of the other is constantly monitored. A radical alienation from one's own desire is established and one becomes a proper victim for the ideological forces of the culture industry which plays to our weak self-images and promises power and fame to those who buy into the consumerist system.

Not only advertising, but television and cinema in general, are indicted by the prevalence of the narcissistic character. The tendency to take up an external stance toward oneself is reinforced by the approval showered on media stars. The modern child's countless hours of TV-watching naturally trains him/her to adopt an external stance totally dissimilar to the one recommended by our analysis of decision making, that is, grasping one's situation objectively *for oneself*. Once one has become an object for others, the step to masochism or sadism is not difficult to understand. The narcissist, depending on factors of development such as class, gender, race, and attractiveness, adopts a masochistic or sadistic position, or wavers between the two.

One may speculate that the predominance of the *masochistic* attitude would predispose one to live out a series of painful decisions abruptly to end involvements. Good things or potentially gratifying accomplishments are taken away from the self by the cruel other in one's own psyche. The sadistic decider, on the other hand, would hardly see decisions as an issue and would commonly make controlling decisions about others' lives. At the same time, the latter would probably suffer from an inability to close off options for fear of not becoming the great Everything that draws constant approval. If these are actually primary aspects of modern individuality, it is not at all difficult to understand the widespread preoccupation with identity and authenticity. If I *exist* only in the eyes of others, and I feel most like myself when I am acting out desires constituted by those controlling others, it is no wonder that questions like "Who am I?" "What is the meaning of my life?" "What am I supposed to become?" "What is my true self?" are so difficult to answer.

Hegel's master-slave dialectic

Important aspects of narcissism and sadomasochism are prefigured by an allegory presented in Hegel's (1807) *Phenomenology of Mind*. The allegory of the master and the slave reveals a dialectical structure in self-consciousness that is quite helpful in grasping the movement of the deciding psyche. (Our reading of the allegory draws on interpretations by Marcuse, 1941; Hyppolite, 1946; and Kojève, 1947.) In working through this section, it will be helpful to imagine that the entire allegory refers to an "internal" psychological struggle, much as Freud's id-ego-superego model is generally portrayed.

The allegory begins with an attempt to conceptualize the emergence of human self-consciousness out of animal (or human infantile) existence. Hegel notes that an important component of this process would involve sensation and the satisfaction of desire. The animal or infant consciousness is absorbed in the world and is not able to reflect on itself, to say "I." The human subject works through language to position itself as the source of desire. For example: "*I* am the one who is restless and hungry." "*I* am the one who had better run from that lion." Hegel thus asserts that self-consciousness is inextricably interwoven with desire.

What are the implications of associating desire and self-consciousness so intimately? If consciousness of self is precipitated by a sense of desire, then a sense of the unity of the self ("self-certainty") requires a destructive or negative relation to objective reality. Anything which is *other* is perceived as a threat. It must be dominated or destroyed. At the simplest level, our desires are satisfied in this process of negation. The apple is consumed and our hunger is satisfied.

But the certainty of self that emerges from the repetitive satisfaction of desires is not a solid one. The objects consumed disappear from the world and the sure existence of self that was sensed in the process of consumption fades as well. The dependency of self-consciousness on objects in the world begins to be intolerable. The human thus begins to seek an object which is not destroyed as it is negated. This would have to be another something which is actually nothing – in short, another self-consciousness.

To clarify: in desiring an object, the "I" that desires equates itself with the object. In the moment of desiring, the "I" is merely the desire of that object and nothing else. Yet self-consciousness longs to be something greater than the objects it operates on; it senses that it is an entity that transcends objectivity. It must move toward a non-natural object in order to be directed toward itself. This non-natural object would have to be another self-consciousness. The unity and certainty of one's own self-consciousness can only be affirmed through recognition by an other self-consciousness. From this idea, Hegel, and later Lacan, derive the notion that the "I" is established as the *desire of the desire of the other*. "The vocation of man – to find himself in being, to make himself be – is realized only in the relation between self-consciousnesses" (Hyppolite, 1946, p. 167).

With this background, the plot of the master-slave dialectic is established. Hegel asks us to assume that we are witnessing the "first" encounter between two humans. This is obviously not an actual historical situation, but rather an event which is prototypical. Our two humans, rather than being able to recognize each other as fellow human beings, as equal and autonomous self-consciousnesses, take each other as objects. A life-and-death struggle for the recognition of the other ensues. Each being attempts to impose himself on the other, to force recognition from him. The struggle gradually moves toward the death of one of the participants. The stronger of the two does not wish to kill the other, however. To do so would defeat his purpose. He seeks to be inserted into the opponent's desiring consciousness as the supreme value – to become the desire of the other. One of the combatants must surrender his own desire in order to recognize the desire of the other. Thus, in fear of actual death, a compromise is realized in which the weaker becomes slave to the stronger, the master.

The master believes he has accomplished a number of aims in the struggle. He is recognized as existing only for himself. The world of objects is at his command through the mediation of the slave. He enjoys the products of another's work. He does not need to work, nor deal with the natural world directly. His self-consciousness, he believes, is free from dependence on nature. He lives only to negate objects in a continuous search to shore up his own self-certainty. And he is supreme not only in his own eyes but also in the eyes of a potential equal.

The slave appears to be the slave of the master, but he is actually the slave of *life*. He would not risk life for freedom. He is thus doomed to arranging the world as the master requires and must subordinate his own satisfaction. He is forced to defer gratification in order to serve the master. Labor becomes his way of life, requiring that he operate continually in the world of objects. He is unable to live as if he were an entity independent from thinghood. He is in fact a thing himself, a mere object in the eyes of the master.

The master's initially enviable state actually constitutes an existential impasse. The recognition he sought from an equal is unattainable from the lowly slave. His apparent independence from the natural world masks his real dependence on the slave. All he touches has the mark of the slave on it. He is constantly reminded of his own contingent existence. He knows nothing of fending for himself. Without the slave, he would be nothing.

This paradoxical situation has a dialectical structure. In its internal contradiction, Hegel (and, later, Marx) finds the potential for a positive development. The consciousness of the slave has been established in a manner that holds the promise of true autonomy. His understanding of the world has developed in direct relation to the natural world. The slave sees that he is the agent who transforms the world. He learns through his labor that the world can be changed. His activity is preserved in the things he works on; he sees his selfhood objectified in his products. Furthermore, the slave is acquainted with the fear of death. He has become aware that he can relinquish his attachment to life in order to attain greater ends. He begins to have a vision of a world in which individuals would be mutually recognized and autonomous through collective work toward the fulfillment of common needs.

In the modern world, however, the slave's consciousness is so mutilated by his experience that he is unable to manage the revolt which would free him. The master suffers, too, because his existence is dependent upon slavery. His humanity is only partial and is corrupted from within by the fact that his accomplishments are not his own. They are achieved only through limitations posed on others.

"... living people have become bits of ideology" (Adorno, 1966, pp. 267–8)

A backdrop for the concept of ideology is now in place. Essentially, the concept shifts the locus of self-deception from the isolated psyche to the social relations in which subjectivity arises. Ideology entails a certain practice of representation and mode of signification (meaning-creation) that sustains the illusion that the subject is the origin of his/her activity and is entirely responsible for it. Ideology is not "in the mind." It is a set of social relations, the maintenance and management of which requires a character-based complex of misrepresentations of self and world. Ideology refers to a system in which prevail a psychic slavery for the majority and a false sense of mastery for a few.

Drawing freely on the imagery of the master-slave dialectic, we can relate ideological processes to issues in deciding. Rationalization flows from the position of the master. The master is weak and has to justify in some manner the superiority of his interests. Rationalizations are not self-evident – they attempt to justify a relation of inequality that has no logical basis. The master leans on the threat of violence to sustain his favored position. In the internal movement of deciding, anxiety over self-disintegration forces the subject into a subjected position under the rule of an unconscious stereotype.

Sherry, for example, as she tried to decide not to begin her affair, actually becomes sick – she "stopped her whole program." The stereotype insisted on satisfaction and the more rational parts of her self, even while realizing that the act might be self-destructive, or at least a dangerous gamble, had to go along. This part that "goes along for the ride" is figured in the slave (and is paralleled in Freud's notion that the ego serves three harsh masters – the id, superego, and external reality). The anxiety of the slave over his precarious existence generally inclines him to go along with the master's commands and demands. But, as the slave grows toward the accomplishments Hegel mentions (work, recognizing self in his products, etc.), his sense of inalienable rights is augmented. In the deciding consciousness, this occurs when the command of the stereotype is challenged, when the false grounds for dominion are exposed, and when the organization of the social world is no longer seen as natural. The slave-subject approaches autonomy in these moves – and, we should note, if he has actually understood autonomy, he will not seek to take up the position of the master.

Ideology thus refers to a complex system of subjections. These must be negated if a decision is to be seen as rational in any sense. These subjections include subjection to the past through the operation of stereotypes and "conscience"; subjection to the requirements of the current practical situation; and, subjection to contemporary rationales provided by everyday social discourse.

These modes of subjection function simultaneously to chain the individual ideologically. The outcome is that we tend to cave in, "sell out," and surrender to the structure of societal pseudo-reality. This is the opposite of freedom, as Adorno argues:

> A free man would be one who need not bow to any alternatives, and under existing circumstances there is a touch of freedom in refusing to accept the alternatives. Freedom means to criticize and change situations, not to confirm them by deciding within their coercive structure. (Adorno, 1966, p. 266)

By definition, ideology plays a central role in the maintenance and reproduction of a particular organization of society. The various character styles that we develop in the process of socialization, because they are also forms of unfreedom, tend to contribute to prevalent ideological processes. To establish this hypothesis adequately would require another book, but we have already seen a number of life histories that document this idea. For example, Nathan's life course (Chapter 9) demonstrated a characterological disposition to become anxious in situations where he is recognized for accomplishment by an external (or internalized) master and to back away from these nascent achievements. This disposition meshes neatly with a social trend of dubious merit.

Consider a clipping from a magazine published primarily to advertise apartment furnishings and the associated jetset lifestyle. The article is entitled, "The New Job Psychology: Rather Switch than Fight? Changing Careers is the '80's Work Ethic." There is nothing inherently problematic with career changes, particularly if acquired skills build on one another, yet the institutionalization of job-hopping is difficult to justify. It serves only the interests of corporations seeking to have the most effective individual in the right place at the right time – with no respect for the needs of individuals or work communities.

Individuals in western society tend to personalize problems at work. If something goes wrong, or they get too tired, or they find no satisfaction in what they do, they imagine that the problem lies within. After all, others are not complaining – they're glad to have a job. The switching, shifting, and moving to new locations associated with the "new job psychology" has the effect of reinforcing the structure of existing jobs. "Someone else will gladly take your place if you can't handle it." And when that person has been damaged by the inhumane structure of the job, he or she can move on, too.

The individuals caught up in this process are likely to attribute their relocations to personal growth: "I had outgrown that job. I needed to expand my horizons." But they forget the insecurity they experienced, the friendships that were disrupted, and the seniority they lost. Marcuse hit it on the nose: "everyday reality . . . is mystified in its institutions and relationships, which make necessity into choice, and alienation into self-realization" (1978, p. 54).

The article on job-hopping ignores this dimension of the career change phenomenon. It sustains the rationale of the ideological process:

> Increasing numbers of men and women in their late 20s and 30s are tantalized by the idea of switching careers. As recently as the 1960s career changes – especially for professionals – were generally regarded as a sign of incompetence or mental instability. Today, a switch in careers is regarded as just another reasonable choice.

Nathan's personal struggle has been aggravated by popular rationalizations for stereotyped impulses of exactly the sort he would like to comprehend and transcend. The public mind forgives itself for what its economic system must do – in this case, because the interest in rapid corporate development is seemingly best served by transfusion of fresh blood. The personal costs of these patterns are now coming to light. The pain and emptiness "at the top" have been well-documented (Wolman, 1973; Kovel, 1981), but it will take more than private resistance (e.g., refusals to be transferred) to alter this and many similar ideological processes. It will take more than collective fascination with the lives of those who choose to step off the beaten path. In a surrealist story, "Notes on a Useless Country," Georges Hénein captures the horrifying contemporary scene:

> Close to the frontier, the ground loses its consistency. There banks of quicksand absorb, with greedy lips, dozens of desperate people every day. These quicksands are a sort of official institution; to forbid or modify their use would seem a sacrilege.
>
> They are edged with well-beaten paths where, a contemplative look on their faces, tourists take up position, equipped with folding chairs and supplies of food. From time to time, these spectators make comments in a low voice, respectfully, on the exceptionally pathetic physiognomy of a suicide.   (Hénein, 1975, p. 95)

Deciding revisited

One interest predominates in our concern with the social context of major life decisions: the perpetuation of authoritarian and oppressive social relations through the impact of ideology on the deciding consciousness. It must be clear that we are employing the term *ideology* in a manner that deviates from the colloquial usage that refers merely to a system of beliefs (as in "Islamic ideology"), or to a set of political ideas (as in "capitalist ideology"). A critical use of the term has watered down its original sense in the Marxist context (as a system of beliefs that justifies the favored position of the ruling class), but recent American and European scholarship restores the original meaning and focuses attention, as we have, on the affective, behavioral, material, and social-structural components of ideological processes (cf. Barratt, 1984; Earnest, 1982; Thompson, 1984; Coward and Ellis, 1977). Ideas and beliefs alone would be insufficient to make people "love their chains" as they currently do. In connection with this broader context, we can review quickly our point of view on the psychological moment of ideology.

To a certain extent, relations of domination feel natural and acceptable because the master-slave relationship lies at the foundation of all self-consciousness. At moments of heightened self-consciousness such as those that involve decision making, sadomasochistic structures are especially insistent. They contribute powerful images of what feels like "exactly the right thing to do" in perfect accord with either a slavish or masterly mentality. But as Hegel's allegory demonstrates, neither state is sufficient. Both modes of consciousness are seriously limited. The path toward autonomy from stereotyped and ideologically determined decisions must lie in other modes of self-projection. That ideal direction would require neither violence to one's own interests, nor the subjection of another to one's power (as in any form of "identification with the aggressor").

Over and over again, we have seen that needless and painful starts and stops in central life involvements mimic the images of domination that saturate modern consciousness. Mary, who suffered abuse in two marriages and in the workplace, now attempts to become the master-millionaire herself. Bill submits to corporate guidelines and has to take on even more work in a repetition of the power his mother wielded in the household, making it difficult for him (like his own father) to be the father he would like to be. Karen sets off to find a home, cutting herself off from community roots, seemingly in fear that she might replicate her sister's suicide were she to stay. Sherry is ready to retire from this hostile world into a warm cave. Nathan hides his disappointment about possibilities for meaningful work in this society under a jargon that masks the violent socialization he suffered.

How may we know that a particular decision is guided by an ideological consciousness? According to Geuss' (1981, pp. 13–22) general description of "false consciousness," it is necessary to scrutinize a variety of rationalizations that figure in the deliberation leading to a choice, including:

1 presentation of value judgments as statements of fact
2 portrayal of a social phenomenon as a natural one
3 depiction of one's own interests as the interests of the social whole
4 legitimation of domination
5 obfuscation of social contradictions intersecting in the individual life
6 adoption of collective rationalizations ("systems of beliefs or attitudes accepted by agents for reasons or motives those agents *could not* acknowledge", p. 20).

The implications of this perspective for decision making are obviously extensive. Our inquiry has brought us only to the threshold of the problem of ideology. But, having begun with a naive phenomenology of deciding, perhaps this in itself is an accomplishment. And judging from the fact that current psychological models remain totally oblivious to the ideological penetration of cognitive processes in general, the accomplishment seems greater still.

From our current vantage point, it is possible to make a limited number of fragmentary observations relevant to the role of ideology in major life decisions:

It is probable that we need to pay much more attention to aspects of current living that are rarely subjected to decision making, that is, rarely problematized. Are these unquestioned areas zones which the slavish mentality has occupied totally? For example, do we really need to work 8–10 hours a day, when unemployment rates run so high? From another angle, what are we *not* inclined to be making decisions about? What are we not encouraged to deliberate about?

To what extent is our ability to choose constrained by what can actually be chosen? Objective social structures shape life possibilities directly. We tend to focus on opportunity, on pathways through the obstacle course of life. We rarely challenge the placement of the obstacles.

How much does deciding in the modern world require a relatively arbitrary construction of identity? Roland Barthes writes: "You are a patchwork of reactions: Is there anything *primary* in you? Any classification you read provokes a desire in you to put yourself into it somewhere: Where is your place?" (1977, p. 143). Given that we must take up positions in social roles, can we find justifications for choosing one role over another? Do we merely hop from identity to identity, from ideological discourse to ideological discourse, as Lifton (1969) and Henriques and colleagues (1984) have argued?

Do major life decisions often boil down to matters of personal finance and status? A friend told me that "ninety-nine percent of decision making is what you choose to purchase or put your money behind. Your spending habits are your way of casting a vote for the way you want society to be, for what it should provide and produce." A neglect of the extent to which spending decisions shape everyday life, especially as our small choices totalize in the social sphere, is clearly a denial of the determining power of the economic sphere. The problem also appears in the fact that life chances are severely constrained by lack of access to capital. Furthermore, personal identity and one's social function are intertwined in an especially confusing manner: making a living today requires an exchange of "self" for "money." Under the requirements of advanced industrial society, we all become prostitutes (or pimps). Only a privileged few can even pose the question, "What will I work at? What do I want to do? What is worth doing?"

Often decision problems stem from not knowing what sort of society one is up against. How can the nature of social reality be known? Mao Tse Tung provides the beginning of an answer in his 1937 essay "On Practice":

> If you want to know a certain thing or a certain class of things directly, you must personally participate in the practical struggle to change reality, to change that thing or class of things, for only thus can you come into contact with them as phenomena; only through personal participation in the practical struggle to change reality can you uncover the essence of that thing or class of things and comprehend them.

Personal troubles/public issues

Western culture and its psychologists idealize the autonomous individual, the self-actualizing personality, and the independent person. Our deconstruction of typical decision problems unveils these ideals as ideology. The privatization of choices allows domination and oppression to proceed unchallenged. The "autonomous" individual all too often shuns engagement and purposeful collectivity, and falls back on the pseudo-collectivity of mass spectator events to fill the empty spaces in everyday life. True mutuality and interdependence would threaten the thin armor that narcissism provides.

Individualistic values may be considered as a necessary moment in development toward meaningful living, but they should be viewed only as temporary shelters on the road to full engagement with the struggles of one's era. Decision problems and dilemmas do not disappear in the life of the collective, engaged subject; they may, in fact, be more painful and difficult for such an individual. As problems are confronted directly, rather than symbolically – as social rather than personal – long-standing relations of domination are disturbed. The stress entailed by direct confrontation may, however, be mitigated by the possibility of human solidarity against systematic and unnecessary suffering.

BIBLIOGRAPHY

Abt, L. E. and Weissman, S. L. (eds) (1976) *Acting Out*, 2nd edn New York: Aronson.

Adorno, T. W. (1938, 1982) On the fetish-character in music and the regression of listening, in A. Arato and E. Gebhardt (eds) *The Essential Frankfurt School Reader*. New York: Continuum.

Adorno, T. W. (1966, 1973) *Negative Dialectics*. New York: Seabury.

Adorno, T. W. (1973) *The Jargon of Authenticity*. Evanston, Ill.: Northwestern University Press.

Adorno, T., Frenkel-Brunswick, E., Levinson, D., and Sanford, N. (1950) *The Authoritarian Personality*. New York: Harper.

Allport, Gordon W. (1955) *Becoming: Basic Considerations for a Psychology of Personality*. New Haven, Conn.: Yale University Press.

Althusser, L. (1969) Freud and Lacan, in *Lenin and philosophy*. New York: Monthly Review.

Atchley, R. C. (1975) The Life Course, Age Grading, and Age-Linked Demands for Decision Making, in N. Datan and L. H. Ginsberg, *Life-Span Developmental Psychology: Normative Life Crises*. New York: Academic Press.

Balint, M. (1959) *Thrills and Regressions*. London: Hogarth.

Barratt, B. B. (1984) *Psychic Reality and Psychoanalytic Knowing*. Hillsdale, NJ: Analytic Press.

Barthes, R. (1977) *Barthes by Barthes*. New York: Hill and Wang.

Basing, M. K. (1977) *The Art of Life*. Austin, Tex.: University of Texas Press.

Bayley, N. (1963) The Life Span as a Frame of Reference in Psychological Research. *Vita Humana, 6*, 125–39.

Benjamin, W. (1978) *Reflections*. New York: Harcourt Brace Jovanovich.

Bergler, E. (1949) *The Basic Neurosis: Oral Regression and Psychic Masochism*. New York: Grune and Stratton.

Bergmann, Frithjof (1977) *On Being Free*. Notre Dame, Ind.: University of Notre Dame Press.

Bernard, Jessie (1981) The Good-Provider Role: Its Rise and Fall. *American Psychologist, 36*, 1–12.

Bernstein, R. J. (1971) *Praxis and Action*. Philadelphia, Penn.: University of Pennsylvania Press.

Bernstein, R. J. (1978) *The Restructuring of Social and Political Theory*. Philadelphia, Penn.: University of Pennsylvania Press.

Binswanger, L. (1963) *Being-In-The-World*, trans. Jacob Needleman. New York: Basic Books.

Bleicher, J. (1980) *Contemporary Hermeneutics*. London: Routledge & Kegan Paul.

Block, J. (1971) *Lives Through Time*. Berkeley, Calif.: Bancroft.

Boss, Medard (1963) *Psychoanalysis and Daseinsanalysis*. New York: Basic Books.

Brammer, L. M. and Abrego, P. J. (1981) Intervention Strategies for Coping with Transitions. *The Counseling Psychologist, 9*, 19–36.

Bridges, William (1982) *Transitions: Making Sense of Life's Changes*. Reading, Mass.: Addison-Wesley.

Brown, N. O. (1959) *Life Against Death*. New York: Vintage.

Clark, Ronald W. (1980) *Freud: The Man and The Cause*. New York: Random House.

Cohen, John (1964) *Behavior in Uncertainty and Its Social Implications*. London: George Allen and Unwin.

Collins, Douglas (1980) *Sartre as Biographer*. Cambridge, Mass.: Harvard University Press.

Conway, Flo and Siegelman, Jim (1978) *Snapping: America's Epidemic of Sudden Personality Change*. New York: Dell.

Cooper, David (1970) *The Death of the Family*. New York: Vintage.

Cornman, J. W. and Lehrer, K. (1968) *Philosophical Problems and Arguments: An Introduction*. New York: Macmillan.

Coward, R. and Ellis, J. (1977) *Language and Materialism: Develop-*

ments in Semiology and the Theory of the Subject. London: Routledge & Kegan Paul.

Craib, I. (1976) *Existentialism and Sociology.* New York: Cambridge University Press.

Crystal, J. C. and Bolles, R. N. (1974) *Where Do I Go From Here With My Life?* Berkeley, Calif.: Ten Speed Press.

Dahrendorf, Ralf (1979) *Life Chances.* Chicago, Ill.: University of Chicago Press.

de Beauvoir, Simone (1952) *The Second Sex.* New York: Knopf.

du Bos, Charles (1962) Meditations on the Life of Baudelaire, in H. Peyre (ed.) *Baudelaire.* Englewood Cliffs, NJ: Prentice-Hall.

Earnest, W. R. (1982) *Work and Its Discontents: The Ideological Containment of Social Contradictions.* Unpublished PhD dissertation, University of Michigan.

Eisenstein, Zillah R. (1979) *Capitalist Patriarchy and the Case for Socialist Feminism.* New York: Monthly Review.

Erikson, E. (1963) *Childhood and Society.* New York: Norton.

Fenichel, O. (1945) *The Psychoanalytic Theory of Neurosis.* New York: Norton.

Ferenczi, S. (1919, 1976) On the Technique of Psycho-Analysis, in M. S. Bergmann and F. R. Hartman (eds) *The Evolution of Psychoanalytic Technique.* New York: Basic Books.

Ferenczi, S. (1928, 1976) The Problem of Termination in Analysis, in M. S. Bergmann and F. R. Hartman (eds) *The Evolution of Psychoanalytic Technique.* New York: Basic Books.

Fingarette, H. (1969) *Self-Deception.* London: Routledge & Kegan Paul.

Fingarette, H. (1974) Self-Deception and "The Splitting of the Ego," in Richard Wolheim (ed.) *Freud: A Collection of Critical Essays.* New York: Anchor.

Florence, Jean (1978) *L'Identification dans la théorie Freudienne.* Brussels: Facultés Universitaires Saint-Louis.

Freire, Paolo (1970) *Pedagogy of the Oppressed.* New York: Seabury.

Freud, A. (1937) *Ego and Its Mechanisms of Defence.* London: Hogarth.

Freud, S. (1900, 1951) The Interpretation of Dreams, *Standard Edition*, Vol. 4. London: Hogarth.

Freud, S. (1909a, 1951) Analysis of a Phobia in a Five-Year Old Boy, *Standard Edition*, Vol. 10, 22–152. London: Hogarth.

Freud, S. (1909b, 1951) Notes upon a Case of Obsessional Neurosis, *Standard Edition*, Vol. 10. London: Hogarth.

Freud, S. (1911, 1951) Formulations Regarding the Two Principles in Mental Functioning, *Standard Edition*, Vol. 12, 213–26. London: Hogarth.

Freud, S. (1913, 1951) The Disposition to Obsessional Neurosis. A Contribution to the Problem of Choice of Neurosis, *Standard Edition*, Vol. 12, 311–26. London: Hogarth.

Freud, S. (1914) Remembering, repeating, and working-through, *Standard Edition*, Vol. 12, 153. London: Hogarth.

Freud, S. (1920, 1951) Beyond the Pleasure Principle, *Standard Edition*, Vol. 12, 3–66. London: Hogarth.

Freud, S. (1925, 1951) Negation, *Standard Edition*, Vol. 12, 235–42. London: Hogarth.

Freud, S. (1940, 1951) Splitting of the Ego in the Process of Defence, *Standard Edition*, Vol. 23, 271–8. London: Hogarth.

Fromm, Erich (1941) *Escape from Freedom*. New York: Holt, Rinehart and Winston.

Fromm, Erich (1947) *Man for Himself*. New York: Holt, Rinehart and Winston.

Gabel, J. (1975) *False Consciousness: An Essay on Reification*, trans. M. and K. Thompson. New York: Harper and Row.

Gear, Maria, Hill, M. A., and Liendo, E. C. (1981) *Working Through Narcissism*. New York: Aronson.

Geuss, Raymond (1981) *The Idea of a Critical Theory: Habermas and the Frankfurt School*. Cambridge: Cambridge University Press.

Gould, Roger (1978) *Transformations*. New York: Simon and Schuster.

Goulet, L. R. and Baltes, P. B. (eds) (1970) *Life-Span Developmental Psychology*. New York: Academic Press.

Gregg, G. G. (1982) *Structures of Selfhood*. Unpublished PhD dissertation, University of Michigan.

Grossman, Richard (1978) *Choosing and Changing*. New York: E. P. Dutton.

Gutknecht, D. and Meints, J. (1982) Social Ruts: Emergence and Resolution of Intrapsychic Conflict. *Free Inquiry in Creative Sociology*, 10, 159–62.

Guttmann, D. L. (1964) An Exploration of Ego Configurations in Middle and Later Life, in B. L. Neugarten (ed.) *Personality in Middle and Late Life*. New York: Atherton.

Habermas, J. (1968, 1971) *Knowledge and Human Interests*, trans. Jeremy J. Shapiro. Boston, Mass.: Beacon.

Habermas, J. (1976a) *Communication and the Evolution of Society*. Boston, Mass.: Beacon.

Habermas, J. (1976b) Systematically Distorted Communication, in P. Connerton (ed.), *Critical Sociology*. New York: Penguin.

Hawkes, T. (1977) *Structuralism and Semiotics*. London: Methuen and Berkeley, Calif.: University of California Press.

Hegel, G. W. F. (1807, 1967) *The Phenomenology of Mind*, trans. J. B. Baillie. New York: Harper and Row.

Heidegger, Martin (1927, 1962) *Being and Time*, trans. John Macquarrie and Edward Robinson. New York: Harper and Row.

Held, David (1980) *Introduction to Critical Theory: Horkheimer to Habermas*. Berkeley, Calif.: University of California Press.

Hénein, G. (1975) Notes on a Useless Country, trans. J. H. Matthews, in J. H. Matthews (ed.) *The Custom House of Desire*. Berkeley, Calif.: University of California Press.

Henriques, J., Hollway, W., Urwin, C., Venn, C., and Walkerdine, V. (1984) *Changing the Subject: Psychology, Social Regulation, and Subjectivity*. London: Methuen.

Holt, R. R. (1962) Individuality and Generalization in the Psychology of Personality. *Journal of Personality*, 28, 377–404.

Horan, J. J. (1979) *Counseling for Effective Decision Making*. Belmont, Calif.: Wadsworth.

Horkheimer, Max (1972) *Critical Theory: Selected Essays*. New York: Herder and Herder.

Husserl, E. (1948, 1973). *Experience and Judgment: Investigations in a Genealogy of Logic*, trans. J. S. Churchill and K. Ameriks. Evanston, Ill.: Northwestern University Press.

Hyppolite, J. (1946, 1974) *Genesis and Structure of Hegel's Phenomenology of Spirit*. Evanston, Ill.: Northwestern University Press.

Hyppolite, J. (1966) Commentaire parlé sur la *Verneinung* de Freud, in J. Lacan, *Ecrits*. Paris: Seuil.

Izenberg, Gerald N. (1976) *The Existentialist Critique of Freud*. Princeton, NJ: Princeton University Press.

Jacoby, R. (1975) *Social Amnesia*. Boston, Mass.: Beacon.

James, William (1890, 1918) *The Principles of Psychology*, Vol. 2. New York: Holt, Rinehart and Winston.

Janis, I. L. and Mann, L. (1977) *Decision Making: A Psychological Analysis of Conflict, Choice and Commitment*. New York: Free Press.

Jay, Martin (1973) *The Dialectical Imagination: A History of the Frankfurt School and the Institute of Social Research, 1923–1950*. Boston, Mass.: Beacon.

Kafka, F. (1914, 1974) *I Am a Memory Come Alive: Autobiographical Writings*. New York: Schocken Books.

Kernberg, O. (1977) *Object Relations Theory and Clinical Psychoanalysis.* New York: Aronson.

Kojève, A. (1947, 1969). *Introduction to the Reading of Hegel.* New York: Basic Books.

Kovel, Joel (1981) *The Age of Desire: Case Histories of a Radical Psychoanalyst.* New York: Pantheon.

Lacan, J. (1966) *Ecrits.* Paris: Seuil.

Lacan, J. (1968) *The Language of the Self: The Function of Language in Psychoanalysis.* Baltimore, Md: Johns Hopkins University Press.

Langan, T. (1961) *The Meaning of Heidegger.* New York: Columbia University Press.

Laplanche, J. and Pontalis, J. B. (1973) *The Language of Psychoanalysis.* New York: Norton.

Lasch, Christopher (1979) *The Culture of Narcissism.* New York: Norton.

Laughlin, H. P. (1979) *The Ego and Its Defenses.* New York: Aronson.

LeMaire, A. (1977) *Jacques Lacan,* trans. D. Macy. London: Routledge & Kegan Paul.

Lévi-Strauss, C. (1966) *The Savage Mind.* Chicago, Ill.: University of Chicago Press.

Levinson, D. (1978) *The Seasons of a Man's Life.* New York: Knopf.

Lewin, Kurt (1964) *A Dynamic Theory of Personality.* New York: Holt, Rinehart and Winston.

Lifton, R. J. (1969) *Boundaries: Psychological Man in Revolution.* New York: Vintage.

Loevinger, Jane (1976) *Ego Development.* San Francisco, Calif.: Jossey-Bass.

Lorenzer, A. (1976) Symbols and Stereotypes, in P. Connerton (ed.) *Critical Sociology.* New York: Penguin.

Lowenthal, M. F., Thurnher, M. and Chiriboga, D. (1976) *Four Stages of Life.* San Francisco, Calif.: Jossey-Bass.

Lundin, Robert W. (1969) *Personality, A Behavioral Analysis.* New York: Macmillan.

Marceil, J. C. (1977) Implicit Dimensions of Idiography and Nomothesis: A Reformulation. *American Psychologist, 32,* 1046–55.

Marcuse, H. (1941) *Reason and Revolution: Hegel and the Rise of Social Theory.* Boston, Mass.: Beacon.

Marcuse, H. (1955, 1962) *Eros and Civilization.* New York: Vintage.

Marcuse, H. (1970) *Five Lectures: Psychoanalysis, Politics, and Utopia.* Boston, Mass.: Beacon.

Marcuse, H. (1978) *The Aesthetic Dimension: Toward a Critique of*

Marxist Aesthetics. Boston, Mass.: Beacon.

Marx, K. (1964) *Economic and Philosophic Manuscripts of 1844.* New York: International Publishers.

May, Rollo and Ellenberger, H. F. (eds) (1958) *Existence.* New York: Basic Books.

Mayman, Martin (1968) Early Memories and Character Structure. *Journal of Projective Techniques and Personality Assessment, 32,* 303–7.

Menaker, E. (1979) *Masochism and the Emergent Ego,* ed. Leila Lerner. New York: Human Sciences Press.

Merleau-Ponty, M. (1945) *Phénoménologie de la perception.* Paris: Gallimard.

Miller, G. A., Galanter, E., and Pribram, K. H. (1960) *Plans and the Structure of Behavior.* New York: Holt, Rinehart and Winston.

Mitchell, Juliet (1975) *Psychoanalysis and Feminism.* New York: Vintage.

Navratil, M. (1954) *Les Tendances constitutives de la pensée vivante,* Vol. II. Paris: PUF.

Neugarten, B. L. (ed.) (1964) *Personality in Middle and Late Life.* New York: Atherton.

Neugarten, B. L. (1975) Adult Personality: Toward a Psychology of the Life Cycle, in W. C. Sze (ed.) *Human Life Cycle.* New York: Aronson.

Paci, Enzo (1963, 1972) *The Function of the Sciences and the Meaning of Man.* Evanston, Ill.: Northwestern University Press.

Palmier, Jean-Michel (1969) *Lacan: Le Symbolique et l'imaginaire.* Paris: Editions Universitaires.

Pascal, Roy (1977) *The Dual Voice.* Totowa, NJ: Rowman and Littlefield.

Poster, Mark (1975) *Existential Marxism in Postwar France.* Princeton, NJ: Princeton University Press.

Rangell, L. (1969) Choice Conflict and the Decision-Making Function of the Ego. *International Journal of Psychoanalysis, 50,* 599–602.

Read, Herbert (1963) *The Contrary Experience: Autobiographies.* New York: Horizon Press.

Reich, W. (1945, 1972) *Character Analysis.* New York: Simon and Schuster.

Reich, W. (1972) *Sex-Pol: Essays, 1929–1934.* New York: Vintage.

Ricoeur, Paul (1950, 1966) *Freedom and Nature: The Voluntary and the Involuntary,* trans. E. V. Kohan. Evanston, Ill.: Northwestern University Press.

Ricoeur, Paul (1970) *Freud and Philosophy: An Essay on Interpreta-tion*. New Haven, Conn.: Yale University Press.

Riegel, Klaus F. (1975) Adult Life Crises: A Dialectic Interpretation of Development, in N. Datan and L. H. Ginsberg (eds) *Life-Span Developmental Psychology: Normative Life Crises*. New York: Academic Press.

Rose, Gillian (1978) *The Melancholy Science: An Introduction to the Work of Theodor W. Adorno*. New York: Columbia University Press.

Rovatti, Pier A. (1973) Critical Theory and Phenomenology. *Telos*, 15, 25–40.

Royce, Joseph R. (1982) Philosophic Issues, Division 24, and the Future. *American Psychologist*, 37, 258–66.

Sartre, J.-P. (1956) *Being and Nothingness*, trans. Hazel Barnes. New York: Philosophical Library.

Sartre, J.-P. (1960) *Critique de la raison dialectique*. Paris: Gallimard.

Sartre, J.-P. (1968) *Search for a Method*, trans. Hazel Barnes. New York: Vintage.

Sartre, J.-P. (1972) *Plaidoyer pour les intellectuels*. Paris: Gallimard.

Schacht, R. (1970) *Alienation*. New York: Anchor.

Schlossberg, N. (1981) A Model for Analyzing Human Adaptation to Transition. *The Counseling Psychologist*, 9, 2–18.

Seidenberg, R. F. (1972) The Trauma of Eventlessness. *Psychoanalytic Review*, 59, 95–109.

Sennett, R. (1970) *The Uses of Disorder*. New York: Vintage.

Sennett, R. (1980) *Authority*. New York: Vintage.

Sève, Lucien (1978) *Man in Marxist Theory and the Psychology of Personality*. Atlantic Highlands, NJ: Humanities Press.

Shainberg, David (1973) *The Transforming Self*. New York: Intercon-tinental Medical Book Corp.

Shapiro, D. (1965) *Neurotic Styles*. New York: Basic Books.

Shiff, Richard (1978) Art and Life: A Metaphoric Relationship, in Sheldon Sacks (ed.) *On Metaphor*. Chicago, Ill.: University of Chicago Press.

Silvestre, Michel (1979) Mise en cause de la sublimation. *Ornicar?*, 19, 11–30.

Spence, Donald T. (1982) *Narrative Truth and Historical Truth: Meaning and Interpretation in Psychoanalysis*. New York: Norton.

Steichen, Edward (1963) *A Life in Photography*. New York: Double-day.

Stekel, W. (1949) *Compulsion and Doubt.* New York: Grosset and Dunlap.

Terkel, S. (1980) *American Dreams: Lost and Found.* New York: Pantheon.

Thompson, J. (1984) *Studies in the Theory of Ideology.* Berkeley, Calif.: University of California Press.

Tversky, A. and Kahneman, D. (1974) Judgment under Uncertainty. *Science, 185,* 1124.

Tversky, A. and Kahneman, D. (1981) The Framing of Decisions and the Psychology of Choice. *Science, 211,* 453–8.

Van der Sterren, H. A. (1966) Life Decisions During Analysis. *International Journal of Psychoanalysis, 47,* 295–8.

Van Kaam, Adrian (1974) Existential Crisis and Human Development. *Humanitas, 10,* 109–26.

Veroff, Joseph (1983) Contextual Determinants of Personality. *Personality and Social Psychology Bulletin, 9,* 331–43.

Volosinov, V. N. (1976) *Freudianism: A Marxist Critique.* New York: Academic Press.

Weisman, A. D. (1965) *The Existential Core of Psychoanalysis: Reality, Sense and Responsibility.* Boston, Mass.: Little Brown.

White, R. W. (1952, 1975) *Lives in Progress: A Study of the Natural Growth of Personality,* 3rd edn. New York: Holt, Rinehart and Winston.

Williams, R. H. and Wirths, C. G. (1965) *Lives Through the Years.* New York: Atherton.

Williams, R. L. and Long, James J. (1979) *Toward a Self-Managed Life Style,* 2nd edn. Boston, Mass.: Houghton-Mifflin.

Williams, Robin M., Jr (1964) Values and Beliefs in American Society, in Michael McGiffert (ed.) *The Character of Americans.* Homewood, Ill.: Dorsey.

Wolman, B. (1973) *Victims of Success.* New York: Quadrangle.

Woodworth, R. S. (1940) *Psychology,* 4th edn. New York: Henry Holt.

Zinn, Howard (1980) *A People's History of the United States.* New York: Harper and Row.

INDEX